twigs

twigs

The Go-Guide to Nesting

JULIA BOURLAND

A Perigee Book

THE BERKLEY PUBLISHING GROUP
Published by the Penguin Group
Penguin Group (USA) Inc.
375 Hudson Street, New York, New York 10014, USA
Penguin Group (Canada), 90 Eglinton Avenue East, Suite 700, Toronto, Ontario M4P 2Y3, Canada
(a division of Pearson Penguin Canada Inc.)
Penguin Books Ltd., 80 Strand, London WC2R 0RL, England
Penguin Group Ireland, 25 St. Stephen's Green, Dublin 2, Ireland (a division of Penguin Books Ltd.)
Penguin Group (Australia), 250 Camberwell Road, Camberwell, Victoria 3124, Australia
(a division of Pearson Australia Group Pty. Ltd.)
Penguin Books India Pvt. Ltd., 11 Community Centre, Panchsheel Park, New Delhi—110 017,
India
Penguin Books (NZ) cnr. Airborne and Rosedale Roads, Albany, Auckland 1310, New Zealand
(a division of Pearson New Zealand Ltd.)
Penguin Books (South Africa) (Pty.) Ltd., 24 Sturdee Avenue, Rosebank, Johannesburg 2196,
South Africa

Penguin Books Ltd, Registered Offices:
80 Strand, London WC2R 0RL, England

PRINTING HISTORY
Perigee trade paperback edition / October 2005

PERIGEE is a registered trademark of Penguin Group (USA) Inc.
The "P" design is a trademark belonging to Penguin Group (USA) Inc.

The Library of Congress has cataloged the original Perigee trade paperback as follows

Bourland, Julia.
    Twigs : the go-girl guide to nesting / by Julia Bourland.
        p. cm.
    Includes index.
    ISBN 0-399-53201-3
    1. Home economics.   I. Title.
TX158.B68 2005
640—dc22   2005043122

PRINTED IN THE UNITED STATES OF AMERICA

10   9   8   7   6   5   4   3   2   1

This book is dedicated to Penelope Blu.

Contents

part one: composing the nest

part two: feathering the nest

10 Signs You're Ready to Nest

1. You're more likely to devour, cover to cover, the latest Pottery Barn catalogue before opening a surprise letter from an ex-boyfriend.

2. You know how to get to the nearest Bed Bath & Beyond and Target without help from MapQuest.

3. Hanging around the house no longer feels like punishment.

4. Knitting no longer seems dorky.

5. Your calls home have more to do with family recipes than unresolved childhood issues.

6. You've bought cleaning supplies in the past month.

7. You know the difference between latex flat and semigloss paint and can wax poetic on the pros and cons of both.

8. You've memorized at least one cookie recipe.

9. You know the difference between a Phillips and a square-tip screwdriver.

10. When friends drop by, they know you'll be home.

Acknowledgments

My books are only as worthy as the thoughts and advice of the women and experts quoted within. Thank you all for opening up your private spaces to me and to the readers of this book. Don't worry, your names and some details have been changed to protect the privacy of your cozy retreat.

A thousand thanks to Joe Veltre for doing the above-the-call-of-duty legwork for finding the perfect home for this book, and to Michelle Howry, for her careful editing and creative contributions. And to my family and friends, thanks so much for all your support and encouragement. Larry and Penelope, you are both magnificent nesting mates (even when the laundry gets out of control). Korki, Cathy, and Liz, I couldn't have written this book—especially during this year!—without your friendship, emotional support, and last-minute baby-sitting. You guys are the best.

twigs

Introduction:
Why I Wrote This Book

Confession: I have not always been a nester. In fact, I spent most of my early twenties avoiding anything that had to do with domesticity—from personalizing my college dorm room (a blur of a memory consisting of hospital-white walls and requisite Matisse poster) to decorating my first shared apartment, a run-down Victorian flat in San Francisco's Chinatown. My entire collection of furniture consisted of a futon bed and a block-and-board bookshelf. My clothing was more likely to be found draped over a doorknob than hanging neatly in the closet. And any plant I dared purchase had the typical life span of two weeks.

But when I turned twenty-six and moved into my first studio apartment (a sun-flooded nest with cute built-ins and bathroom tile from the 1920s), something shifted. For the first time in my life, I began to take pride in my living space. Perhaps it was due to my change in status—I was finally living alone, and it felt so powerfully adult. But I believe it reflected an emerging desire for a more restful, inspiring, rejuvenating home life—since my social life seemed overwhelmingly busy at the time, I had just been promoted at work and my responsibilities were increasing, and I had begun taking on freelance writing assignments in my spare time.

Upon moving in, I removed the mildewed sliding plastic doors affixed to the tub and hung a rod and shower curtain instead. I took off the doors of the kitchen cabinets, painting over the bare spots where the hinges had lain for so many years, to open up the space and show off my new dishware (one of my first "adult apartment" purchases). A friend gave me some leftover yellow and orange nasturtium blossoms from her terrace garden, which I planted in tiny terra-cotta pots and lined along my kitchen windowsill. And at a used bookstore, I picked up my very first cookbook, *Great Recipes from the* New York Times, which remains a fixture in my kitchen today.

That whitewashed studio was like a first love. Looking back, I mainly remember its romantic attributes, the good times, and how it made me feel every time I stepped foot in the door—peaceful, inspired, restored. I rarely recall its lesser qualities: the landlord-mandated (stained) white carpet covering an otherwise perfect hardwood floor, a radiator that hissed every night around 2 a.m., and my next-door neighbor's neon flashing I LOVE JESUS sign, onto which my bay windows looked. The apartments that followed never quite lived up to the charm and seduction of my first. There's something about a first love or a first home that evokes the sensual.

Nesting, or turning your living space into "home," is a sensual experience, or should be for those of you yet initiated to the notion that a cozy home life can lead to creative, inspired, and enriched living. Creating a living space that allows you to let down your guard is an essential ingredient to happiness.

With crazy work schedules, social and familial obligations, hateful errands, and that incessant need to squeeze in all those things you want to do—exercise, take art classes, volunteer, find and nurture true love—building a nest where you can retreat, rejuvenate, and inspire your senses with pleasing colors, sounds, scents, and textures is one of the most basic ways to keep in touch with your creativity, which really is keeping in touch with yourself.

For those of you who are familiar with my previous two books, *The Go-Girl Guide: Surviving Your 20s with Savvy, Soul, and Style* (Contemporary Books, 2000), and *Hitched: The Go-Girl Guide to the First Year of Marriage* (Atria Books, 2003), you already know what interests me as a writer: empowering women through various stages in life. The "nesting" stage comes to women at different times—moving into a first "adult" apartment, moving in with a lover, and starting a family being the most common phases in life when the nesting instinct hits. For some women, though, it never arrives at all, which I think is a missed opportunity for inspired living. We all work too hard at our careers and relationships to not indulge in a sensual home life.

The past couple of years I've been knee-deep in fixing up a "fixer," and I've learned a thing or two about what it takes to transform a house or apartment into a "home." I've included my observations and experiences within *Twigs*, but the tips and advice extend far beyond my own. In writing, I interviewed more than sixty women who live around the country and combed through their secrets and tips on ways they have transformed their apartments, condos, and houses into cozy nooks. Most of the women I spoke with were referred by colleagues and friends who knew I was writing this book and seeking interviews with natural "nesters."

When I was in doubt about a certain nesting conundrum that came up over and over again in my discussions with these women—how to arrange furniture in a room with five doors and no wall space, for instance—I gathered thoughts and suggestions from professional decorators and design gurus. I also threw in a few Nesting Pleasures to indulge in the next time you are itching to unplug your phone and curl up inside your nest with no one but yourself (and maybe your cat) to enjoy your sensual surroundings. Look for those scattered about the book.

Feel free to skip around the chapters to whatever subject inspires you. If overflowing closets are ruffling your feathers, thumb directly to Chapter 3 for advice on lightening the load. If you can't bear to look at that faded fabric covering your favorite chair, skip ahead to Chapter 6 and read all about slipcovers or having the piece reupholstered.

Whether you're just out of school and nesting in your first adult apartment or are settled but inspired to create a more cozy home, *Twigs* has everything you need—including inspiration for motivation—to compose the nest of your dreams. So nestle on back into that cozy sofa of yours (we'll talk about choosing this in Chapter 2 on page 34) and imagine the possibilities. Your nest awaits a transformation. And so do you.

part one

Composing the Nest

Arranging the Pieces

Not particular about location, the House Finch uses whatever nesting materials it finds—paper scraps, cellophane, dried grass, mud.

 Like most nesters, I loathe moving. Except for one aspect—the empty rooms. An empty room resonates with sensual appeal: the echo of bare foot slapping floorboards, unfiltered light from unshaded windows splashing across unadorned walls, the smell of newly waxed floors and possibly fresh paint.

I like to think of empty rooms as the bare branches of a tree or the vacant tips of telephone poles upon which we build our nests. Going with this analogy, the building in which we dwell is merely the location of our roost. Some dwellings, of course, have better views, more natural light, and sexier surroundings than others, but that's a separate matter (and who said life was fair?).

The true essence of a nest is not the tree or abandoned chimney top where it rests, but the twigs and grasses of which it is made—our belongings and the way we weave them together. That's the good news for those of us nesting inside an airless basement flat—especially one rented with a no-paint policy.

Arranging our belongings in a tapestry that encourages relaxation, rejuvenation, and connecting with others—the heart of sensual living—is the first step toward turning "a place to live" into a home.

weaving our twigs

What turns a bare room into a cozy retreat? Lighting and textures have something to do with it, and we'll get to those concepts later in the book. But I would argue that what really creates mood within a given space is the weave of its belongings, our "twigs," and how they relate to each other and walls surrounding them.

Interior designers all approach furniture placement differently, following certain guidelines for rhythm, harmony, scale, and balance. If you're into feng shui, there's a whole spiritual side to arranging furniture, too. But you don't need a master's in design or Buddha's blessing to create sensual spaces in your home. Just keep the following five principles (in the following order) in mind.

principle one: determine the primary use of space

Before you decide what goes where, ask yourself how you want to use the room, advises San Francisco interior designer Jennifer Puhalla.

"Sometimes my clients try to do too much in one room," she says. "So we first determine how to use the space. Then, we decide what furniture makes sense to include. A lot of times, there is too much stuff crammed into a room and we need to reduce what we have and only keep the essentials."

Consider the small living room that attempts to feature a seven-foot sofa and several chairs for entertaining—along with a giant media center and, say, a home office. Such arrangements lead to a cramped, cluttered, even junky-looking nest.

Determine your primary goal for the space, then build your nest using only the furnishings that help accomplish that goal, moving the rest of your twigs into other rooms (or zones, for those in studios) . . . or to the local Salvation Army.

Deciding use of space usually requires compromise. In the living areas, for instance, ask yourself if you want to prioritize entertaining or creating a sensual zone for your postwork and weekend rituals.

Entertaining

If entertaining is most important, you'll want to build a nest that welcomes others. Comfortable seating is critical, as is a place to serve meals. With entertaining as the main priority, it's important to cluster your belongings in patterns that encourage conversation. A sofa, for instance, might have a couple of chairs to its side (think of an L-shape configuration) and a coffee table in front for snacks, beverages, and board games. The TV needs to hang out near your bed or in a less prominent part of the room. Unless, of course, all you do when you entertain is watch TV, but that's none of my business.

Relaxing

If you'd rather weave a nest that appeals to your personal pleasures, arrange your belongings so that they accommodate your ideal method of relaxation. Perhaps that means featuring The Sacred Yoga Mat and meditation pillows in the main living area, placing the love seat and coffee table in a quiet corner to the side. Or, arranging your belongings in relation to a prominently placed long wooden table designated for sewing and art projects.

For Madison, twenty-eight, from Westfield, New Jersey, nesting begins with the act of unwinding. The one thing she looks forward to most when coming home after a busy day is her armchair. So, her living area proudly features The Chair, which faces the TV and sits next to a stack of her newest magazines. Reading and vegging out in front of the tube helps her unwind every time.

principle two: use the architecture of a room as a focal point

So advises Carole Talbott, author of *Decorating for Good: A Step-by-Step Guide to Rearranging What You Already Own* and mastermind of the design technique she has coined "Visual Coordination," which involves placing furniture in relation to the room's architecture.

"The first thing I do when I walk into a space is read the shape of the room and the shape of the walls. Then I select the architectural focal point within that space," she says. It is around this architectural focal point that Talbott begins to weave a pattern of furniture so, as she puts it, "the structure of the room and its contents become one."

Common architectural focal points include windows, fireplaces, an arched doorway, an alcove, a built-in bookshelf—typically, the most dominate structural feature that draws your attention when you enter the space. The feature might not be as obvious as a fireplace, though. It could be an exposed brick wall in an otherwise square, plastered room. Or, deco-styled light sconces accenting the top of one wall. An ancient radiator spanning the length of one side of the room might also be its only focal point, God help you. Whatever it may be, its critical in determining the placement of your twigs, says Talbott.

The idea behind her approach is to balance your belongings with the given architecture, creating an organic, sensual harmony when you walk into the space. By creating this balance, your belongings blend in naturally, creating a visual harmony that turns an ordinary space into one with ambiance. A fireplace, for instance, serves as a natural focal point for a main seating arrangement, say, a sofa, which should face the architectural interest, coupled with a chair or two, and perhaps a coffee table.

To balance the room's sensual offerings, place the main seating ensemble so that it faces the architectural feature. Putting the sofa flat against the brick wall, which may feel instinctive, for instance, creates a sensual imbalance in the room, since the heaviest belongings would be smashed up against the wall that's already rich with texture and color.

In fact, one of the biggest mistakes people make in arranging their furniture, says Talbott, is nestling the sofa into the architectural focal point rather than addressing it. Positioning the sofa and/or chairs so they face a set of windows instead of backing into them is a more balanced arrangement, because the heavier belongings won't add to the weight of the wall that bears the main architectural interest. Instead, they balance the room by adding visual interest to the area that lacks it. Besides, this setup also provides the opportunity to gaze out of the windows when sitting, rather than have your back against the glass.

Determining the main architectural feature isn't always a no-brainer. For instance, many rooms and studios have more than one architectural feature around which one might compose a nest. A bowling-alley-shaped loft may have a wood-burning stove on one end and a floor-to-ceiling wall of glass on the other (a girl can dream, can't she?). Or, a tiny living room might have one wall sporting a fireplace, and an opposite wall with picture windows and a view. Or, a room may take the shape of an L, opening up the possibility for more than one nest within the space.

"If you have two focal points within a space, you need to choose one," advises Chris D'Alessio Gay, an interior designer in Colorado Springs, Colorado. "One is always more dominant than the other," she says. Use that one as an anchor for the main seating arrangement, then build a smaller nest addressing the secondary point of interest. If a fireplace is competing with a view, for instance, decide which focal point is more important to you. If you want the view for entertaining, place the main seating arrangement facing the windows, then put a couple of cozy armchairs facing the fireplace for quieter contemplation.

In some cases, it may be possible to angle a sofa or seating setup so they address both focal points. This is, in fact, how I've arranged the nest in my living room. With a fireplace flanked by built-in bookshelves on one wall of our living room and picture windows facing a view of the San Francisco Bay on another, I've angled the sofa to address both. I've also placed a leather armchair and ottoman facing the view, allowing for quieter nesting in that space.

Not every room boasts an architectural feature you want to necessarily highlight prominently, and if your nest fits into this category, do not fret. You'll actually have more freedom of arrangement than the rest of us. All you need is one inspiring piece of furniture or artwork or sculpture to act as a magnet around which your other belongings may gravitate. Cluster your main seating arrangement facing a beloved tapestry hung on the wall for a textured and colorful view.

principle three: weave your belongings one twig at a time

Start with the largest or heaviest piece of seating furniture, placing it so it addresses the architectural focus in the room, suggests Talbott. "That establishes the pattern. The rest of the furniture fits in around this anchor piece like pieces of a puzzle," she says. "The idea is to put the room together one piece at a time, pragmatically. In this way, you don't really have a choice on where things go—the placement is perfect to the space."

For example, in the living room, the most important piece is usually the sofa. "The sofa anchors the room. It's a functional piece," says interior designer Puhalla. Once you've determined its placement, the rest of your twigs—the side tables, additional chairs, bookcase, desk, TV, and plants—can be positioned in relation to that main piece. "The rest of the furniture falls into place in the remaining space," says Puhalla, "since it's easier to see what space is left over for other things—two side tables and a lamp, for instance, or just a sconce on the wall."

A pleasing setup in the living room, for example, is to place a small table in front of the sofa, and a chair or two either to the sofa's side, creating an L shape for seating, or to simply angle a chair toward the sofa so that the two address each other. In the bedroom (or sleeping zone for those in studios), place a bureau, armoire, or chair on the adjacent wall to the bed to balance the space. In the dining area, anchor the zone with a table, then balance out any remaining empty spaces with whatever you have—a freestanding china cabinet, bookshelves, even a potted tree.

If you have a very small living area, start with the items that build the nest you most desire within the space. For instance, in a studio, if your entertaining area is most important, start weaving your nest with a love seat and chair addressing the focal point. Once that arrangement is in place, you can figure out which areas in the room are left for the bed and possibly a dining nook which can double as a work space for your laptop. If, on the other hand, a dining atmosphere for entertaining is what you find most sensual to your nest, establish the placement of your table first, then weave in the rest of your belongings around that most important piece.

For those living in the luxury of space with separate bedrooms, the bed is a natural place to begin when weaving the nighttime nest. Once you've picked that placement, which is usually best set against your largest, most empty wall—not pushed up into the bay windows—then you can decide where to put the chest of drawers or wardrobe and your other pieces.

As you begin filling in the room, keep in mind two additional balancing acts: height and weight. For optimal balance, you'll want to vary the heights of your furniture around the room, so all of your tall pieces—bookshelf, floor lamp, floor-to-ceiling mirror—don't end

Always position a table next to your chairs—especially if the chair is cozy. That way, you will avoid knocking over your glass of wine or cup of tea after you have set it on the floor and forgotten about it. Also, you won't have to get up to fetch your beverage every time you want a sip.

up on one side of the room, with your horizontal pieces—sofa, consoles, benches—dominating the other.

And, you'll want to avoid placing all your tall pieces on the wall that sports three door frames, giving that side of the room all the vertical perks. That could give you neck strain every time you step into the room.

"Mix the scale of your belongings," advises interior designer Puhalla. "Balance out your larger items with smaller pieces. This gives a room more interest. If everything is the same size and shape, then nothing is important in the room. Not every piece of furniture has to be The Piece you're in love with."

principle four: use the space, not just your walls

A common arrangement for those in tiny spaces is to stash all the furniture against the wall, leaving the middle of the room void of belongings. I have been guilty of this in many of my previous apartments, but once I broke through that habit and began moving furniture out into the room (my dining-room table sits in the middle of our dining nook, instead of flat against the wall, and our sofa-seating arrangement floats out from the wall, giving depth to that side of the room, I realized that space was meant to be used, not stared at.

"Pulling furniture away from the wall gives a room depth and forces you to weave through a room rather than just walk though empty space," explains interior designer Gay. "Weaving through a pattern of furniture creates comfort and coziness in a room. It feels more natural than walking through a room in which all the furniture is lined up against the walls. Winding your way through a room feels like walking down a path in a garden."

Besides, when you pull furniture out into the room—a seating cluster here, a chair and lamp there—you have space behind those larger belongings for other twigs, such as a potted plant, or a console

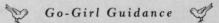

Go-Girl Guidance

For those of you in the thick of renovation or who are about to move into a new place to nest (and have the opportunity to think about wall space—or the lack thereof), consider furniture placement before you grab the wrecking ball and jackhammer.

Kristen, twenty-seven, from Greenville, South Carolina, and her husband figured out the placement of their furniture before they moved into their home, and got a builder to put an electrical outlet on the floor in the exact spot over which their couch would stand. That way, they can plug in a lamp in the middle of the room by the side of the sofa without running the cord across the floor to an outlet on the wall.

table for displaying pictures. In that way, it actually can expand the space you have—even in a tiny room.

For those with limited wall space due to such built-ins as a fireplace, doors, and giant windows, there may be no other option than to bring your belongings out into the open. Meryl, twenty-nine, from Oakland, California, suffers from lack of wall space. In her living room, one wall is filled with bay windows, and two doors chop up another. Coils of heaters fill every corner of the room, making that space unusable, and two of the walls come together at a forty-five-degree angle (what to do there?).

Her only option was to pull the furniture away from the walls about two to three feet. Not only is a cohesive seating arrangement viable, but bringing her furniture out into the room enables her to walk behind the furniture from one door to the other, eliminating a traffic problem she otherwise encountered. Which leads me to the last point.

principle five:
consider traffic

Always allow a space of at least two feet between clusters of furniture. Around doorways, try to leave at least three feet of empty space in the vicinity to eliminate that cramped feeling upon entering a room.

If you find yourself walking sideways or always knocking your knees to get between the mini-nests you have composed around your home, the arrangement is too cramped for the space, and you must either try another arrangement or get rid of some of your stuff.

NESTING PLEASURES:
REARRANGE YOUR ROOMS
(ON PAPER FIRST, PLEASE)

As you consider the concepts in this chapter, model your options before rolling up your sleeves (and breaking your back!). This will give you a bird's-eye view of your nesting potential.

Materials:
Measuring tape
Pen
Graph paper
Ruler (if you want to be particular about it)
Scissors

1. Measure the length and width of the room you wish to rearrange. Draw the same dimensions on a piece of graph paper (one square on the graph paper equals one square foot.) Use a ruler for extra-straight lines. Don't forget to indicate where doors and windows are—measure the widths of these, too, for accuracy before marking them on your graph.

2. Measure the length and width of all the furniture you have for this room. On another sheet of graph paper, sketch these dimensions. If an object you have is circular or oval, measure the longest and widest points, mark them on the graph paper, then draw in the shape freehand as best you can.

3. If the "furniture" is big enough, write on the cutout what the piece is (unless it's obvious to you). Or, shade in the

shapes with different colors or patterns—stripes, solid, diagonal lines, dots—so they'll pop out on the page.

4. Cut out the pieces of furniture, then have fun arranging them atop your mock room. With everything drawn to scale, you'll have an easy time checking for such composition concerns as balance, whether your main piece addresses the main architectural focal point, as well as whether or not your arrangement allows the mandatory two-foot distance between pieces (that's two squares apart on your mock-up).

Note: While this modeling can give you some ideas, it is only two-dimensional, and therefore won't indicate if you've balanced furniture heights in the new arrangement. You won't know that until you actually move your furniture around (not advisable to do alone).

If you live solo, invite a friend or two over to help. Stock the fridge with imported beer or fancy soda, and snacks for motivation. Order takeout for lunch, too. Hospitality is critical when asking for backbreaking favors.

If you must attempt the rearrangement alone, remember to lift from your legs, not your back. And if you have hardwood floors, protect them from scratches by placing washcloths beneath the legs of heavy bureaus, chairs, even your bed frame. The furniture glides right across the floor with very little effort.

By the way, don't feel like your first attempt at furniture placement has to be The One. Reese, twenty-nine, from Cleveland, Ohio, for instance, has rearranged her furniture about six different times over the course of three years. Finally, she found a pattern that works for her nest. Eventually, you will, too.

on discouraging spaces

We all have them. What follows are several common complaints and solutions worth trying.

"There's a Coffeemaker in My Bedroom!"

The open floor plan is the bane of studio dwellers (or the bonus, depending on how you look at it). Some nesters love the openness of their studios and feel that very quality is what makes their abode so cozy.

Before her current studio, Brice, twenty-six, from Chicago, lived in a one bedroom. Because she didn't own massive amounts of furniture to fill up the space, the apartment seemed bare and cold to her. In her current studio, she has created a dining zone and living area in the main space, and has placed her bed in the corner. The design was a success—friends always invite themselves over for drinks before they go out, she says.

The open floor plan is not without drawbacks, though. It's a fine art to create distinct areas or moods within a large open space without establishing a choppy, blocky setup. One solution is to use screens to help define the spaces. Lana, twenty-nine, from Los Angeles, has designed several for her open floor plan. For one screen, used to separate her kitchen and dining areas "so visitors can't see how I destroy the kitchen every time I have a party," she took seven cheap three-by-one-by-one boards purchased at the Home Depot, painted them dark ivy green to match the walls of the living/dining room, and attached hinges to the long sides, forming a vertical accordion divider. Then she sponge-painted them with a metallic version of the same ivy green and hung framed four-by-six-inch pictures of her travels from a length of grosgrain ribbon secured to the top of each board.

Nita, thirty, from Los Angeles, used a curtain to divide space in her nest. "My studio is one main room with an extremely wide separate hallway that leads to the kitchen from the front door," she explains. She decided to make the hallway her "bedroom," since it was wide enough for a queen-sized bed. She hung a curtain up so guests entering her apartment are trafficked into the main room. Many guests never even notice that the front hallway is actually a bedroom, she says.

Careful clustering of your furniture can also divide the space into different uses while preserving the openness of a studio. This is how Amanda, twenty-seven, from Chicago, composes her living area, which she describes as "a big box." To make space for dining in this room, so her official dining room could function as a home office, she placed her couch across the center of the room, using it as a visual division between the seating and dining areas. "The couch helps define the dining space without closing off the room or making it feel smaller," she says.

Kate, twenty-nine, from Grand Rapids, Michigan, uses the same technique in her living room, which is long and narrow. "Instead of putting the couch against the wall, we have it going across the width of the room, about three-quarters of the way in," she says. "This makes our hang-out space more square. Then behind the couch in the less used space, we put a bookcase and a table to display things on. We also hide the baby jogger back there."

When creating clusters of mini-nests within an open space, interior designer Puhalla recommends keeping some degree of unity between the subdivided areas. For instance, stick with the same color scheme throughout the studio. Window coverings should remain uniform around the room.

If you use furniture to help divide the space, consider pieces that you can see over or through, like a backless bookshelf dividing a living area from a dining zone. That way, you'll create two distinct spaces but still keep the room airy, since you can see through the piece into the other area.

"There Is No Room to Roost!"

Living in tiny spaces can be the coziest nesting of all, but not without meticulous planning. For starters, it's critical that you keep the nest tidy and organized, advises Abby, twenty-six, from Woodbury, Connecticut, whose past nests have included shared apartments and a studio. "That's the key to living in small spaces. I make my bed everyday, for instance," she says. "Without the clutter, you feel like there's room to relax and enjoy the space."

Meryl, twenty-nine, from Oakland, California, lives by the same motto: She has a place for everything she owns so her small home is orderly and manageable. "It's like putting a puzzle together," she says. In addition to keeping tidy, Meryl also swears by furniture with wheels. Both her TV stand and coffee table are on casters, making them easy to roll out into the room when needed, then moved to the side when she needs room to spread out. Bonus: It makes cleaning a whole lot easier, she says.

Madison, twenty-eight, from Westfield, New Jersey, and her mate use tray tables for dining, since their living space is too small for a table. They pull them out while eating, then fold them up when they're done.

Another trick to living in small spaces is to use your furniture for more than one purpose. Leah, thirty-six, from Wichita, Kansas, doubled up her dining-room table as an oversized work desk when she lived in tiny quarters. When guests came over, she'd clear off her work and pull the table out into the middle of the room for formal dining.

And speaking of dining-room furniture, you're probably familiar with the practice of pulling out the chairs around the table for guests in the living room. To pull the look together, consider getting chairs that complement the look and feel of your living room setup. So advises Carissa, thirty-five, from Chicago: "We have dining-room chairs that match the living room, so they can be pulled in when we need extra seating."

Roomie Advice

Share tight communal space? Alice, thirty-four, from San Diego, and her fiancé came up with this compromise: "I have a special reading chair and light in the living room next to the TV. When my fiancé wants to watch sports or whatever, he uses wireless headphones. That way, we can both use the room at the same time."

"There's a Pipe the Size of Manhattan in My Nest!"

Many of us have adorable nests except for the One Obvious Blight—stained wall-to-wall carpet, exposed water pipes in the corner of the living room, a floor-to-ceiling electric heater circa 1970 in the center of your living-room wall. When you are not able to rectify the situation due to a lease or the high cost of renovation, your only recourse is to either hide the blemish or distract from it, so it's not the dominant feature of the room.

Isabelle, thirty-one, from Sacramento, California, has a metal fuse box and transformer on the main wall of her living room. "To add insult to injury," she says, "the boxes are huge and about three feet off the floor so you can't really hide them with pictures." Her solution: She concealed the feature with a piece of cream-colored cloth that matched the walls. "You don't see the boxes anymore," she says, admitting that she's not sure the cloth is any better.

An ugly pipe can be painted the same color as the walls to blend them into the room—just be sure to use an enamel water-based paint, because it dries harder than the typical acrylic latex-based paint. A hideous heating system can be shielded with a tall silk screen carefully placed in front when it is not in use.

Ripping up stained carpet and refinishing the floors beneath it (assuming they are hardwood and worth the effort) is one option for that common blemish, but if your lease doesn't allow for that, take a tip from Sally, twenty-nine, from New York City. She strategically placed throw rugs over the "awful shag carpeting" that covers her apartment.

Lana, twenty-nine, from Los Angeles, also has a discouraging feature to contend with: "My living room has the ugliest fireplace in

America," she says. "It's a black hole in the wall." To distract the eye, she hung over the top and sides of the opening a handmade arched bough of dried botanicals, including magnolia pods, that she collected.

For Hannah, thirty-four, from Van Nuys, California, the small bathroom that the previous owner had carved out of a closet is her one grudge. Because the WC lacks an outside wall, there was no way to punch out a window and make the room less tomb-like. Her solution was to paint the room a sunny yellow and hang a salvaged, multipaned wood window on the largest wall to trick the eye into thinking there was a real window there. She plans to ask her artist brother-in-law to paint a faux garden on the wall behind the "window" to enhance the visual trickery.

If the object of your disgust can't be cloaked, consider a distraction—an oversized painting in colors that scream for attention placed on the opposite wall, a sculpture or potted tree in front of said offense, even spot lights, angled in the opposite direction, will direct the eye away from the blight when you enter the room.

Hope, twenty-four, from New York City, cringes when she thinks of the white linoleum flooring in her bedroom. Since she doesn't plan to live in her apartment long, her distraction tactic is to draw attention to the better attributes of the room—her walls and windows. "I have really pretty curtains and have hung one or two nice posters up with lots of photos of family and friends," she says.

As for that hissing radiator, a long chat with the landlord might help. Otherwise, consider a Japanese water sculpture. The trickling sound will at least offer some consistent and soothing white noise, so the crackling and hissing won't come as such a shock at 2 a.m.

"I Live in a Cave!"

A dark, dank apartment that lacks natural lighting is a common discouragement to nesting—at least during the daylight hours when hanging around the house feels like a punishment. Short of maxing out the wattage of every light fixture you own with full-spectrum bulbs that mimic daylight, there's not much you can do to fake natural lighting.

If there is any spot outside of your apartment or home that does get a little sunshine—the entry stairs stoop, a back porch or yard, a fire escape—create a cozy space there, so you can nest outdoors

A New Place to Nest

Happen to be looking for a place to nest? Consider the following most common attributes of a cozy home according to the nesters I interviewed for this book.

- **Natural lighting:** Ideally, your new nest will be oriented toward the south, so light floods your nest throughout the short days of winter, when the nesting urge peaks.
- **Ample storage:** The tiniest homes are often the coziest, in my opinion anyway, unless they are buried in clutter. Garage, attic, or basement storage is an obvious perk to any nest-seeker.
- **A place to garden:** A little plot of dirt, a tiny deck or porch, even a stoop where you can sun yourself while pot-

ting flowers or ivy will give your nest that full-of-life feeling from the inside and out.

- Climate control: It is not possible for a nest to feel cozy if you are sweating bullets or freezing inside. In extreme climates, central air and heat will greatly increase the loungeability of your nest.
- A tub: Every nest needs the small luxury and escape of a bathtub. Also, always test the shower's water pressure before signing a lease. Standing beneath a tepid drizzle every morning is a cruel way to begin the day.
- Laundry facilities: There is nothing more hateful than lugging a heavy wicker basket or bag of dirty laundry down the street for two blocks in order to have clean underwear.

when you feel like being at home, but get depressed by all the darkness.

A tiny bistro table and chair, or simply a few potted plants along the stairs leading to the front door might define those spaces as relaxing spots for sipping coffee or reading the news, allowing you a little light in the mornings or afternoon. If those places don't exist, then you'll have to get your daily fix of sunshine through walks in the morning. Exercise is good for your health, anyway. Right?

At night, the midnight quality of your nest will not be a problem. In fact, it could be an asset in terms of coziness, so concentrate your decorating and design efforts on evening nesting if you live in a cave.

That's how Jeanette, twenty-eight, from Castro Valley, California, deals with her dark apartment. Although it has lots of windows, none of them get direct sun. And the apartment is full of dark, beautiful wood, which adds to the ambiance. Rather than fight the lack of sunlight, she embraces it. She has strung white lights around two of the rooms, and lights candles all around the apartment to accentuate its dark, rich feel. We'll talk more about lighting in Chapter 8, "Lighting," so feel free to skip ahead if lighting problems are the bane of your nesting existence.

2

The Furniture Upgrade

The golden eagle reuses the same nest each year for breeding,
making upgrades and repairs as needed.

 For many of us, the best part of setting up our nest is acquiring the twigs, adhesives, and what-nots that make it our own. However, many of us must face the sad reality that we lack the pre-ferred nesting materials of our dream home.

What many of us have, especially if we've just flown the parental coop, is often a collection of shabby (not chic) belongings: the worn futon sofa/bed, the classic brick-and-board bookshelf, the funky curb-find armchair, the unfinished chest of drawers passed down from a former roommate, and maybe a folding table that we pull out when guests come over for dinner—otherwise, it's the coffee table, baby. It is the eclectic style at its best (and, often, worst).

Acquiring new furniture is an expensive endeavor and no doubt will be a long process. As it should be: Building the nest slowly and with careful planning and foresight creates a unique and sensual look and feel that's hard to achieve (though not impossible) when mass-ordering from Pottery Barn.

What follows is a bare-twigs analysis on winging the furniture upgrade, one twig at a time.

name your style

Nesting materials come in every style. There is the traditional or classical look, consisting of stately, stylized pieces in woods of mahogany, walnut, cherry, and oak. Then there's the provincial look with simple lines, lighter woods of pine and maple, and fabrics of natural fibers in subtle shades.

The modern look brings into the nest clean forms and shiny materials such as steel, glass, and plastics, not to mention bright primary colors. And the eclectic theme picks and chooses from all of the above, keeping at least some aspect of continuity among all the different pieces (more on this in a minute.)

The general rule for the style-conscious furniture gatherer is to simply acquire the pieces you love. Chances are, you'll end up with a collection of twigs that has a common theme—similar lines or colors or wood tones, for instance. Still, a few guidelines will help pull the look together. So keep the following three in mind.

large furniture pieces tend to dictate the "style" of your nest

Because the sofa, the floor-to-ceiling armoire, the bed, and the dining-room table tend to hoard such mass in the nest, these pieces are the first to grab your attention when you enter a room, and therefore, define the style of your nest, intentionally or not.

If you really love a certain style of furniture, but can't afford to buy antiques or the top-of-the-line for every single twig in your nest, concentrate your efforts on at least getting the main pieces in the style you're aiming for. The peripheral twigs are less impressive upon first blink, so if the nesting tables beside your Art Deco couch are from Kmart and are made of cheap wicker, they will most likely fade into the background once set beside your glorious signature sofa.

If your budget won't allow you to purchase the desired stylized versions of these big-ticket items, a less expensive way of establishing a style in your home is to purchase the large pieces in basic Contemporary styles with simple forms and nondescript fabrics. That way, they will fade into the background and your more interesting twigs with distinct styles—the mission-styled recliner chair with ottoman, the Art Nouveau reading lamp, the diner-style Formica breakfast-nook table that you bought for twenty-five dollars at a garage sale—will pop out instead.

Focusing your "style" on the less important pieces is also the way to go if the overall style you're aiming for isn't ideal in terms of comfort. In my craftsman bungalow, for instance, we've aimed for turn-of-the-century simplicity in furniture. However, if you've ever sat on one of the stylized Arts and Crafts sofas, it's painfully obvious that those folks never kicked back to watch a DVD or even read a book on their straight-backed, rigid, narrow settees. So, our sofa is a contemporary Swedish model with simple lines. It seems to fit right in a room with boxy built-ins and rectilinear trim. More important, it's built for comfort.

a "perfectly" coordinated room lacks sensual appeal

This may just be my own personal point of view, but rooms in which all of the furniture are from a single era or style is a room that doesn't give the eye an opportunity to get excited about any aspect of it, because it basically looks the same from every vantage point.

If you're going for a modern style, for instance, having an antique or reproduced Shaker desk in the corner adds visual texture and interest to the room that might otherwise appear sterile and overly uniform in its synthetics and minimalism.

The simple lines of Shaker-styled furniture will not compete with the clean, minimalist forms of modern furniture, so the two styles complement each other in addition to spicing up the room's sensuality. Which leads me to the last point.

with the eclectic look, aim for continuity

This continuity might consist of similar lines, as mentioned in the example above. Or, similar types of wood. A modern orange Lucite coffee table, for instance, might sit jarringly in front of a rococo humpbacked davenport with mahogany cabriole legs featuring lion's claws.

But, a cubic-shaped steel-framed coffee table topped with a slab of polished mahogany that matches the wood of the rococo sofa not only complements the piece, but also adds visual interest with its modern contrast.

Alice, thirty-four, from San Diego, California, followed this guideline when she purchased a cabinet for her dining room. She chose one in the same color of wood as her dining table and chairs. "It makes that part of the room feel like it belongs together," she says.

Back to that bright orange Lucite coffee table: In what type of eclectic setting might that table shine? Imagine it in a Victorian-pink room sitting in front of a cherry-stained wicker settee with big white cushions. Even though the strikingly modern table is at odds with a country-casual sofa, the two complement each other, since they both have red undertones, especially when featured within the pink walls.

the three essential twigs

The act of sensual living requires three bare-bone necessities: a comfortable seating space for friends to gather and converse, a place to sleep, and a table for serving food. Essentially, the three basic needs—eating, sleeping, and connecting with others. Let's discuss these essentials, starting with seating.

The Sofa

There's nothing like a sofa to signify stability and permanence, giving a nest a sense of calm. A sofa defines the purpose of a space—this is where you sit. It's often where guests immediately direct themselves upon entering the room. Partly because the sofa is such an expensive piece of furniture to buy and partly because of its girth—it's usually the largest piece in the living room—a room with a couch is a room that feels settled. And sophisticated. And welcoming. And cozy.

You can entertain several people on a sofa. You can sprawl across one and watch DVDs. You can lounge atop one and devour the latest Hollywood trash in *Us* magazine. And you can host titillating discussions for book clubs, political rallies, or boyfriend-bashing gatherings.

When you have guests spend the night, a sofa offers an additional place to crash—perhaps even for two if you purchase the sleeper-sofa type. And while the futon sofa/bed is certainly convenient for guests, the standard blond-wood frame with a hard foam mattress, is not nearly as comfortable to lounge atop as a real sofa's fluffy cushions—and it reeks (sometimes literally) of college days, no matter how many blankets and throw pillows you use to try to disguise the standard-issue cover. While the futon sofa is certainly an adequate temporary piece to own as you begin to build your nest, if you want your home to really feel adult, retire the futon as soon as your budget allows.

Once you've decided it's time to upgrade to a real sofa, the hard part begins. There is so much to choose from in the sofa department: camel-backed, straight-backed, cushioned, tailored, legless, armless, skirtless, sectionals, love seats, settees, sleepers, and that's not even getting into the fabric choices available—leather, patterned wool, a striped cotton blend.

But before you get hung up on style or fabric options, consider comfort—it's the number one priority, according to Meryl, twenty-nine, from Oakland, California. "Always look for furniture you can lounge on, lean back into, and lay down on," she says. This is her credo. She warns to avoid the too-firm, hard-stuffed pieces that may look sleek and cool during parties, but just aren't comfortable for everyday use. If the goal is sensual living, then comfort is the base of the equation. But what makes for a comfy sofa?

"Everyone has a different body size, so it's important to test out the sofa before you buy one," advises Jennifer Puhalla, a San Francisco–based interior designer. "Bring a book and read a chapter on the sofa you're considering," she says. "See how easy it is to sink into and get comfortable. Make sure when you're sitting upright that your feet touch the floor—sofas that are too tall or too deep can cut off the circulation in your legs."

On the flip side, if you and your partner plan to cozy up together on the sofa in a horizontal position for viewing DVDs (or whatever), assume the position—even if the sales staff gives you the evil eye. It's important to make sure the sofa fits your particular nesting habits. Be courteous, though, and remove your shoes. Then, kick back.

Bounce on it. Stand up and sit down several times in a row using different sitting positions (on the phone, reading, watching TV, doing your bills at the coffee table, taking a sip of wine—just mimic this one—cuddling up with your mate). Rest your arms on the sofa's arms to assess comfortable height, then lie down and rest your head on one to make sure the height is appropriate if the arm is one of your favorite pillows.

Keep in mind that the cushion padding should feel soft on the bum and back, but the springs that support the cushions need to be resilient. And the sofa's frame—sturdy and firm to give your back adequate support. Sofa backs that lean outward slightly will give a more relaxed feel than an upright rigid back. Loose cushions allow slightly more comfort because you can fluff them up and sink into them, unlike the more tailored tight seats and backs that are attached to the frame.

In addition to comfort, you'll want to consider size. It *does* matter. A giant sofa in a small room will dominate the space, leaving very few options for arranging your belongings. In hindsight, Carissa, thirty-five, from Chicago, would have bought two love seats instead of the giant crimson velvet sofa that she currently owns. Although she loves it, "it's hard to make a small room work with a big piece of furniture," she says.

A cozy two-seater love seat or settee is usually sufficient, as long as you have other chairs you can pull in and around the sofa when company arrives. This is especially true because during parties usually only two people sit on the sofa at one time, carefully apart from each other, on either side, arms resting on the sofa's arms—even if the sofa is a three-seater. Of course, if one of your objectives is to have a sofa for friends to crash on, then make sure it's at least long enough to accommodate your tallest friend.

Before purchasing a new couch, carefully measure the space

UPHOLSTERING QUEENS

"I reupholstered a $200 thrift store sofa with a neutral, lightweight—but durable—wool twill. The reupholsterer took off the skirt, replaced the princess pillows with boxy ones, boxified the arms, and raised the back height by six inches. This cost $1,100, but I couldn't have bought a sofa of that size, quality, color, and exact specifications for that price, despite what anybody says."

—Zoe, thirty-three, from Dallas

"If you need to spruce up an old couch, add more batting or foam to the cushions before reupholstering. If cushions tend to droop in the middle, a strong piece of plywood between the bottom of the couch and cushions can work miracles."

—Kasey, twenty-five, from Hoboken, New Jersey

"I had a chaise lounge from my mother that looked old. So when we were putting our new bedroom together, we bought eight yards of fabric, and one afternoon I took out my sewing machine and staple gun and started recovering. It took about four hours and it is now a focal point of our bedroom. It was an incredibly therapeutic and rewarding experience."

—Leah, thirty-six, from Wichita, Kansas

"During college, I found a great upholstered chair for five dollars, but it was pukey yellow and scratchy. So I removed it and made notes on the order and process of reattaching new

> fabric. I changed the arms from straight to rounded by adding two-by-fours and padding. It turned out to be more work than fun, but everyone loved sitting in it and wanted one of their own."
>
> —*Justine, thirty-one, from Mountain View, California*

you've allotted for the sofa and take those dimensions with you while you shop—eyeballing furniture rarely meets with success.

"Lay down painters' tape or masking tape on the floor in the dimensions of the sofa you have in mind so you can really see how the piece will fit the space," advises Puhalla. She also recommends measuring the doorways, elevators, and stairwells through which you may have to navigate to get the sofa into your home. If you discover a tight squeeze, check to see if the legs of your dream sofa unscrew—an extra inch or two can make all the difference in bringing your sofa home.

Once you have the dimensions, the style, and the shape of your dream sofa in mind, it's time to consider fabrics. "Keep it basic, advises Puhalla. "You can always reupholster it or get new slipcovers or throw pillows to liven it up," she says, warning that a fabric too busy or trendy might get old after a few years. A neutral shade will be the easiest to work with, but if you're worried about dirt or stains, a barely striped or checked fabric will help hide blemishes.

Tightly woven wool, cotton, or acetate fabrics are sturdy, stain and tear resistant coverings. Go with what feels most comfortable to your skin and lifestyle. Silk coverings, as gorgeous as they may be, for instance, wouldn't hold up in a nest with two toddlers or one that hosts frequent red-wine sipping gatherings. Leather is one of the most durable coverings for sofas and always looks good, but it is cool to the touch and not the most cozy on cold rainy days during which all you want to do is sink into soft cushions. In general, thick even tight weaves are safe choices.

Last but not least, check the piece for quality before buying. This is good advice whether you're purchasing an antique or going for a sofa straight from the factory. The same criteria may be used for purchasing chairs, too, so look for the following:

- A sturdy frame made of solid kiln-dried hardwood, such as oak, poplar, or maple. Lift one corner of the sofa to assess its heft—heavy equals sturdy. If your purchase has been previously owned, look for evidence of warping or cracking, then walk away if you discover the back of the sofa is droopy.
- Stable legs. These should not wobble when you jiggle the piece. The legs should be either extensions of the frame or screwed in and glued on with additional corner blocks for reinforcement. Double wooden dowels are an alternate indication of quality joinery.
- Strong springs. Lift the cushions and assess the spring system underneath, looking for resilience and strength. The gold standard for sofa and chair spring construction is as follows: "eight-way, hand-tied coil spring construction." This means that each coil spring is hand-tied into place in a series of eight interlocking knots. Quality springs are made of tempered steel.
- Cushions constructed for endurance. Top of the line cushions are made of down feathers, which require frequent fluffing to keep their shape. Foam cushions, made of polyurethane foam or polyester fiberfill are another quality choice. These actually hold their shape better than down-stuffed cushions (look for foam cushions made with a density over 1.8 pounds

per cubic foot). Some foam cushions have extra padding of down to provide additional cush. If the cushions are attached to the frame, a thick padding of burlap or other material should separate the springs from the foam or down stuffing—this will help prevent the popped-spring look years down the line. When inspecting the cushions, don't forget to check that the fabric covering them lines up—especially if it's a patterned sofa.

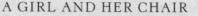

A GIRL AND HER CHAIR

Who knew so many women had a "My Chair"? Here are a few favorites:

"My large velvet Bergere chair with a big cushy matching ottoman with a reading lamp next to it. I sit and read or watch videos while my pug lies beautifully stretched out on my lap."
—*Lana, twenty-nine, from Los Angeles*

"My extra-wide olive-green chair and ottoman in my office—it's perfect for midday naps."
—*Sandra, thirty, from Walnut Creek, California*

"My huge recliner chair in the kitchen. I can look at the backyard in that chair, sit in the afternoon sun that comes in the window, and best of all, fall asleep."
—*Kate, twenty-nine, from Grand Rapids, Michigan*

"My country-style wooden armchair, originally dark wood and now distressed green. The base is very wide and deep, so you can fall back into it. The back is arched, so it's actually comfortable!"

—*Brice, twenty-six, from Chicago*

"My modernistic 1950s-style chair—square beige pillows on a wooden frame. I found it at a garage sale for five dollars."

—*Kate, twenty-eight, from Los Angeles*

"A friend of mine bought a beautiful chair-and-a-half, but after only a few months, their cat scratched a hole in it. So they moved it into the garage, and the dog threw up on it. So they put it in the yard to air out, and it rained that weekend and it was soaked. Naturally, I wanted it. I stripped it down to the bones and recovered it. It looks beautiful."

—*Daisy, thirty-one, from Queens, New York*

Go-Girl Guidance

When applicable, shell out the extra dough and buy the ottoman that matches a chair or sofa—it provides an extra seat when needed and your legs will love you for it, says Nita, thirty, from Los Angeles: "When I bought my sofa, the ottoman seemed like an unnecessary splurge, but I did it, and now I love propping my feet on it while reading or watching TV."

The Bed

What is a nest without a bed? (Preferably one so cozy that you never have insomnia again.) A nest is not a nest until you have a bed that you love as much as (if not more than) your lover.

A peaceful, restful, and welcoming bed is one of the most essential components of composing a nest, and it's amazing how so many of us put that purchase on the backburner until we construct the more public parts of our nest, sleeping restless nights on a hard foam futon that makes all our appendages fall asleep. I'm speaking from experience. I didn't upgrade from the futon to a *real* bed until I was thirty-one years old! Now that I've seen the light, all I can say is: *What was I thinking all those years?*

Twyla, thirty-four, from Dallas, says her bed—a plush mattress with down comforter—is the one thing she always looks forward to after a long day at work. For ten years after college, she had a futon and felt like she was being punished each night.

Olivia, thirty-one, from Berkeley, California, who also finds peace in her bed, always makes an effort to place the pillows and comforter in the morning so that they look "arranged." "Having the bed look neat and clean when I come home after a trip or hard day helps me feel like my life is not totally chaotic," she says. And isn't that what nesting is all about?

In composing The Bed, there are three components to consider: the frame, the mattress, and the bedding. Let's start with the question: to frame or not to frame? It is my opinion that all beds must sit on a frame with a center support if the frame is made of wood, no matter how minimalist that frame may be. This is to preserve the health of your mattress, which absorbs all types of oils and perspiration from you during the night.

Lifting the mattress off the floor helps the air circulate around it, which not only preserves its life, but also keeps your bedroom fresh and airier. Elevating the mattress off the floor also elevates you from floor dust, which makes for a better night's sleep, especially if you have allergies or asthma.

Since the bed typically takes up the most space in a bedroom, the style of frame you choose will dominate the look and feel of your midnight nest. A low-lying minimalist Japanese-style wooden frame will de-emphasize the importance of the bed if, say, your bed is sharing space with an entertaining area, as it might in a studio. Yet, having even a low frame—I'm thinking of those platform-type frames, where the bed rests on a square base with a wide, flat rim, a rectilinear lily pad, so to speak—helps define the bed as a special retreat. More so, at least, than the metal frames with wheels that often come with the mattress and box springs.

A more predominant frame, with head and/or footboard, will add weight and importance to that piece of furniture. (These features also help keep your sheets and blankets tucked in at the bottom, and your pillows from slipping down into the crack between bed and wall at the top.) So, if your bed is the center of your universe and the intended focus of your bedroom (which I suggest it be) and you have the space, keep in mind that larger frames will define the look and feel of your bedroom.

A canopy bed with posts and billowy organza curtains will turn your bed nest into a romantic haven. A sleigh bed of knotty pine gives a bedroom the simple-life look. A leather headboard on a steel frame will give your room a feeling of cool serenity.

When choosing a frame, check for sturdiness (no wobbly legs) and craftsmanship (real wood, not particleboard, and crafted joinery made with double dowel joints braced with corner blocks, for instance, not nails or staples).

While the frame is a largely decorative concern, choosing a

mattress is not. It is the most critical aspect of building the bed nest. It must be comfortable, which in traditional mattresses is a product of the type and amount of padding used in construction. Thick, high-quality padding should be sewn into the mattress in several layers. The more layers, the longer the life. Pillow-topped mattresses offer even more plush to sink into, since these are often filled with down.

Equally important, a mattress must be supportive, which is a product of its innerspring coil system. Industry standards for a basic mattress require that it's made with at least 312 coils of thick wire, but the higher the number of coils, the better. The thicker the wire and the higher the number of convolutions, the more supportive the mattress will be.

Foam mattresses, which are usually made of polyurethane foam or latex rubber, are judged by the density of foam used in the mattress, with the higher densities indicating better quality and a longer life. In assessing quality, check for defined edges and air vents, as well as quality ticking—these will add years of life to the mattress.

When shopping, plan to stretch out on the store models for a good ten to twenty minutes—that's what they are there for. Roll around. Get in and out. Prop yourself up to read. Exhaust your repertoire of sleeping positions. Bring your favorite pillow with you to get the full effect.

Your hips and shoulders should feel well supported, but your limbs should be able to still sink into the cushions. A too-hard mattress will force all your weight onto your hips, shoulders, and other contact points, and tend to cut off the circulation of your arms and legs.

If you share your mattress, be sure to shop with your partner—you'll both want to assess the mattress's roominess as well as its comfort. Have your partner toss and turn on his or her side while you lie on yours. In mattresses with the right amount of firmness, you should not be able to feel every bounce initiated by your partner. If you do, test a more supportive model.

Typically, you'll want at least a queen for two people. A king might even be better if you have the space in your bedroom and there are babies in the future, since crying, teething, and sick babies often end up in the bed. Too much space is easier to rectify than having too little—you can always snuggle up in the middle, but there's nothing worse than feeling cramped in your own bed.

Before you buy, check out the box spring, which is essentially a wooden "box" of additional springs, all covered by lightweight ticking. For best results and longevity, manufacturers advise buying the matching box spring, which is designed to work with the mattress.

Since box springs come in different depths—thick and skinny—you'll want to consider how high you'd like your bed to sit off the floor—if you go with the standard size and your frame already sits several inches off the floor, you may have to literally hop into bed—or at least get a stepping stool. The half-size box spring might bring your bed down to a more reasonable height.

Last but not least: the bedding. If you want to do your bedding right, you'll need to start with mattress pad to protect your fancy new mattress from stains (though I'm not suggesting anything here) and spills. Then, you'll want two fitted bottom sheets—one for the box spring, one for the mattress. Next, a top sheet, a blanket during the winter if needed, and a cover or comforter to top it all off.

Pillows are the final touch, of course, and you may or may not want a dust ruffle to mask the frame. In Chapter 6, "Textiles," look for a long discussion on bedding, from choosing a thread count to picking colors.

NESTING PLEASURES:
REFINISH A TABLE

Materials:
Chemical paint remover or heat gun
Respirator
Sand paper (100 grit, depending on the condition of the wood)
Palm sander (optional)
Mineral spirits and rag
Stain or paint
Polyurethane sealant

1.Remove the old stain or paint. If you are taking off old paint, you may need to strip the paint first using a chemical stripper, which is very messy—use gloves and a respirator—or a heat gun, which produces toxic fumes, respirator required. If you're refinishing an antique, keep in mind doing so may add beauty but will devalue its worth.

2. Sand the piece. This not only removes any paint or stain residue, but also lifts the grains so they are more accepting of a new stain or paint. For large flat surface areas, use an electric sander. Otherwise, plain sheets and elbow grease will do the trick. For previously painted or stained pieces, start with 100-grit sandpaper. You'll need a heavier grit—80 or even 60 grit—if that doesn't smooth the wood enough. If you start with heavier grit, finish off with 100 or even finer—200 grit—which gives the wood a silky smooth finish, like glass.

3. Clean the sanded piece with mineral spirits and a lint-free rag, then let it dry thoroughly.

4. Test the color of stain or paint on a part of the piece that doesn't show—the underside of a table, or the back of a dresser. You'll want practice in applying the finish before you tackle the visible parts, especially if you're using a stain—the amount you apply and the degree you rub it in will affect the overall look and feel.

5. Turn a table upside down, and paint or stain the legs first. Use a clean, lint-free cloth to rub in the desired amount of stain. Follow the grain of the wood, leaving no excess paint or stain pooling on top. Let this dry, then flip the table over and finish the top.

6. Once the piece is dry, decide if you'd like to apply a second coat of paint or stain—perhaps you wished for a darker tone after all. Or, you noticed parts of the table where the paint or stain didn't cover as intended. Test what a second coat does to your "practice" samples from before. Then, apply as you did before.

7. Let the piece dry overnight or longer, until the finish is bone dry and not tacky to the touch. The painted table is now ready to go. If you used a stain, you may wish to paint on one coat of polyurethane sealer to protect the table from water or other liquid stains—especially if the table will receive glasses or food. If you're going for a natural look, choose a non-glossy, matte-finish sealer, which is virtually invisible to the naked eye if you carefully avoid brush marks.

The Table

Last but not least, every nest needs a place to serve a meal. The table is the third staple of nesting. Its presence reveals certain values about the nester—home-cooked meals, lingering conversations, which usually accompany "slow" food, and the very act of sharing food—one of the most sensual and loving exchanges between humans.

You can discuss politics around the table over a lingering bottle of wine following a multicourse meal. You can read the paper at the table while sipping coffee. And when you want to indulge in nesting projects—baking, sewing, scrapbooking, drawing—you have a place to spread out your work. A table is not merely another place upon which you may leave stacks of unopened mail. It is one of the key elements of nesting. Top it with a wooden bowl of oranges (for fresh juice every morning), and your nest instantly assumes a cozier look and feel.

True, not all nests have the space for a long wooden table, which is my personal aesthetic ideal for dining-room tables. In the tiniest of nests, a coffee table may have to double up as serving board, and there is nothing wrong with that. Claire, thirty-five, from Bellingham, Washington, uses her coffee table when serving guests a meal. She uncovered its base in a pile of stuff at an antique store and bought it for $10. Then she paid $100 for a glass top in a frame shop. For best fit, match the height of the coffee table with the sofa's seat. (Occasional tables, on the other hand, should match the height of the sofa's arms.)

Tables with drop leaves make great alternatives for those who live in tiny nests. Most of the time, with the leaves folded down, they can serve as a narrow display table for pictures or a receiving table in the front entryway. When guests arrive for a meal, open the leaves and pull the table out into the middle of the room.

Tables that have detachable leaves also work well for those in tight spaces. Carissa, thirty-five, from Chicago, for instance, has a small oval table with two leaves that she pulls out when company comes over. Not only does the table stay a reasonable size most of the time, but as Carissa points out, "it can 'grow' if and when we ever move into a bigger house."

For best fit in your nest, aim for a table that matches the shape or space of the room. But no matter its shape (oval or square) or substance (wooden, glass, or Formica), a table does not have to be top quality to do the job. After all, you can cover a cheap, collapsible card table with a tablecloth and no one will be the wiser.

Go-Girl Guidance

"When buying furniture, focus on one space at a time until that area is almost done," advises Angela, thirty-four, from Houston, who is renovating her 1907 craftsman fixer-upper. "This has helped us not lose focus, and our mistakes have been more controllable."

---

the pecking order

What comes first, the sofa or the bed? Let me start by saying this: There are two types of nesters—those who want to create a nest for themselves and those who want to create a nest for welcoming others. It is critical to determine which type of nester you most closely identify with before deciding what aspect of your home you want to upgrade first.

Those who are primarily building a retreat for themselves may want to focus their upgrade on the bedroom, since as Nita, thirty, from Los Angeles, puts it: "Go for the bed first, as you will notice the difference for your back immediately." Adds Kate, twenty-nine, from Grand Rapids, Michigan, "The futon definitely goes first. A bed is a good long-term investment. A futon doesn't seem as homey as a real bed."

If, on the other hand, your idea of nesting is creating a welcoming space in which to entertain your friends, you'll likely want to focus your upgrade on the public pieces—a sofa, chairs, a table.

Jessica, thirty-six, from Rome, started the public upgrade soon after tying the knot. "We felt that a nice living room was important to us for entertaining," she says. Katie, twenty-six, from Chicago, also concentrated her upgrade on the entertainment zones: "Couches are a good place to start," she says, "since they take up a good amount of room and seem to be the focal point."

Kira, twenty-six, from Seattle, suggests starting the upgrade with the ugliest pieces you'd like to replace. Her husband has a "heinous" chest of drawers that she will soon try to repaint. "If it doesn't work, then we have a good excuse to get rid of it," she says.

Or, you could try the purge method of upgrade, as advocated by Sarah, thirty-six, from Kailua, Hawaii. "Get rid of everything and start over," she says. "Empty space is better than crap."

how to shop at a flea market

If you're the type to overheat when you walk onto the grounds of a flea market, the following tips will help you scout out the treasures.

Select the Market Carefully

There should be no fleas at flea markets. In fact, there is a whirl of difference between antique flea markets and junky garage-sale-type flea markets, where used motorcycle helmets and defunct hair dryers dominate the "treasures" from which to choose. Avoid the junk dealers of the pawnshop variety markets, and head straight for the quality antique bazaar, the estate or lawn sales in the more posh neighborhoods of your town, and the reputable secondhand antique stores.

Katie, twenty-six, from Chicago suggests scouting out antique furniture stores that are just outside the city lines of larger metropolises—"prices are noticeably thirty to fifty percent higher inside the cities," she says.

Be an Early Bird

If you're going to the flea market with a specific item in mind, you'll want to get there alongside the antique dealers who quickly pick up the quality treasures for sale.

Once there, survey the scene quickly, advises Jasmine, twenty-nine, from Long Island, New York. "First, look to see what they have," she says. "Then look again to see what may go into your house or fit in your car to get home."

If you're uncertain about an item, you *could* hide it under a pile of something until you decide to buy it so other potential buyers won't scoop it up, but I'm not suggesting anything here. (If you do, be sure to replace the item where you found it if you decide not to buy it after all, so the rest of us have a shot at it.)

Go with an Agenda

Veronica, twenty-eight, from Los Angeles, says she's made many mistakes with flea market impulse buys. "It's so easy to get caught up in the process and find something really unique or fun, but then get it home and realize you have no place for it or it doesn't fit into your home at all."

To keep from getting sidetracked, Gretchen, thirty-two, from St. Paul, Minnesota, keeps a file of clever ideas clipped from home décor magazines. Before she goes to a flea market, she browses through the file and makes a list of things to keep an eye out for. Carissa, thirty-five, from Chicago, also keeps certain things in mind when she hits the flea markets—a bathroom mirror, for instance, since she's in the process of redoing that room, or an addition to her cocktail shaker collection.

Always carry measurements of the spaces in which potential furniture pieces will go. If you're looking for a chest of drawers, measure the length and height of wall space in your bedroom where you plan to place the object. If a door or window might interfere with its placement, also measure for depth. Also, take measurements of any doors or stairwell spaces through which you might have to navigate the piece before it rests in peace (or, in one piece).

Don't Forsake All Impulse Buys

Carissa, for instance, once picked up a dark wood frame with an arched Gothic opening and made it into a mirror. "It's truly one of the wildest, neatest things in our house," she says. "I wasn't looking for it, and it's not my style, but if you find something that makes you scream, 'That's fabulous, but I have no idea what to do with it!' just get it. You'll think of something."

Check the Bones

Because flea market finds have gone through several lives with histories of which you will never know, carefully examine the item's "bones"—its frame, shape, and form—looking for cracks, warping, and any other indication of worthlessness.

If the item has a solid, sturdy frame, the ripped upholstery with loose springs can be redone, the peeling paint can be stripped and given a new coat in your favorite hue, the ancient finish can be restained and lacquered (if you're not interested in maintaining its value, since refinishing a wooden antique lowers its worth).

Zoe, thirty-three, from Dallas, for instance, once got a Heywood-Wakefield dresser for $200. "The seller had fifty-seven of them that he had bought from an all-girls' boarding school. He was selling the refinished ones for eight hundred dollars, but this one still was in a scary condition. It took me all summer to refinish, but now it looks great," she says.

"Not everything can go from trash to treasure," says self-described junkyard junkie Magda, twenty-four, from Tiffin, Ohio, who has refurbished several pieces from finds in neighboring alleys. "If a piece has been rained on, is dirty, or you would never even consider it in a store, just let it go. But try to imagine the piece with a new lampshade, a new coat of paint, or with a slipcover." You may be pleasantly surprised by the outcome.

Pay Attention to Displays

Claire, thirty-five, from Bellingham, Washington, found two of her favorite belongings in displays. "I had been shopping for weeks for an armoire at antique stores. Most were over seven hundred dollars, but at one shop, I noticed they were using one for shelving," she says. "I got it for three hundred fifty dollars because the top of one door was a bit warped." She also found a drop-leaf table at a flea market—it, too, was used to display other items.

Think Outside the Dusty Wooden Toolbox

So advises Daisy, thirty-one, of Queens, New York. "The idea is to look beyond the intended purpose of flea-market finds." She's found all types of funky stuff for her nest—a bench from the Hollywood Bowl and an orange seat from a Chinese restaurant. "When people walk in the door, they always stare at the chair and say, 'Is that . . . uh, well, it looks like something from this Thai place I go to.'"

Kate, twenty-nine, from Grand Rapids, Michigan, also uses fleamarket finds for unconventional purposes. Her CD case, for instance, was built for something else in another era (Kate has no idea what its intended purpose was), but she uses the big square thing with dozens of slots to house her music collection.

Olive, twenty-eight, from Boston, is a lover of "found art," so she's always scanning sidewalk trash and flea markets. One of her favorite finds was in the basement trash in her fiancé's apartment building. It was an old wooden window frame, and she uses it as a wall adornment.

Learn How to Haggle

To haggle, one must have cash—$200 in hand, plus your checkbook, advises Kate, twenty-eight, from Los Angeles, a self-described Flea Market Queen. Sally, twenty-nine, from New York City, keeps under $20 in fives and ones in the most visible compartment in her wallet and hides the rest of her cash in an invisible area. When bargaining, she'll say she only has X amount of cash with her and would have to leave to get more. "Vendors never want you to leave," she says.

Gretchen, thirty-two, from St. Paul, Minnesota, always asks, "Is that price firm?" More often than not, they'll suggest a lower price, she says. Persistence also helps. Example: She fell in love with a six-foot wrought-iron arbor and gate marked at $500 at a little antique shop near her nest. Weekly, she stopped by to check the price, which was eventually marked down to $300. In the end, she got it for about $250.

Also, advises Olivia, thirty-one, of Berkeley, California, dress comfortably and low-key. Once while flea-ing, she found an item for $10 and asked if she could pay $7, which would leave her with $3 for a latte. The proprietor told her yes, but as he handed her the item, he said, "The next time you come looking for a bargain, I suggest you leave your Cartier bag and gold necklaces at home." Oops.

Know Your Limits

This goes for spending as well as your energy level. If you can take only one hour of searching through piles of raw fabrics for an antique handmade quilt or through piles of colored glass doorknobs to replace the cheap metallic one that adorns your bedroom door, then focus on finding that particular item when you enter the market and don't get sidetracked by the racks of used leather trench coats—save that for another day.

3

Organizing the Nest

Over two meters long, the Rufous-fronted Thornbird's nest consists of multiple chambers, one built on top of the other.

 In the creed of sensual living, clutter is blasphemy. Clutter breeds apathy toward our living environment. And once apathy storms the nest, it destroys any modicum of sensuality that exists. Stacks of unopened bills on the dining-room table, loose sports equipment in the hallway, old magazines and remote controls on the coffee table, and clothes spilling out of the closet just don't make for a cozy space. Hope, twenty-four, from New York City, puts it simply: "Too much clutter makes me feel like a crazy cat lady."

What follows are suggestions for organizing your clutter in some of the common hotspots in the average nest, starting at the point of entry.

the entryway

The front entrance is tricky because it is a functional component of the nest—it is how you enter and leave. But it's also the first impression you and your guests have of your home . . . and therefore is the *last* place you want to see clutter.

While many of us desire a sensual entryway, with fresh flowers or art to greet us at the door, more often than not, practicalities take over. This area becomes a dumping zone for mail, keys, coats, bags, cell phones, laptops, and for those of us in *that* phase of life, diaper bags and baby paraphernalia. Organization is critical. Let's discuss the essential components for creating sensual order here.

A Place for Coats and Bags

If you are lucky enough to have an entry closet, you may simply hang your hat there, then close the door and not have to look at all the other stuff you've crammed into that space. However, if you live in an old home or apartment, built before closets were in style, you will need to get creative.

In my nest, the front door opens directly into the living room, so there is no transition between the outside world and our private lives. For example, where do we put a coat rack—next to the fireplace? When guests come over, they are at a loss on where to stash their bags and coats, which usually end up scattered about the living room on top of various chairs.

We resolved this problem when we stumbled across a 1920s "coat tree"—one of those old-fashioned entrance pieces consisting of a beveled mirror flanked by coat and hat hooks on either side, all attached to a small table with a drawer and cabinet beneath. It's the perfect fit for our early-century bungalow.

An armoire would have been another option. Sandra, thirty, from Walnut Creek, California, keeps one by her front door and stores such items as coats, boots, mittens, and other junk that accumulates at the entrance. Like a closet, you can close the doors of an armoire and hide the junk, giving your entrance a clean, clutter-free look.

A coat rack is equally useful for holding an assortment of items—purses, coats, umbrellas. Because they are three-dimensional, you're able to cram a bunch of stuff onto them from multiple angles. However, they can give neatniks a heart attack. "My coat rack is always too crowded," says Olive, twenty-eight, from Boston. "It blocks half the hallway and annoys me. Every time I clear it off and put coats in the closet, they seem to spontaneously regenerate on the rack, like limbs on a starfish."

Hooks in the hallway are better space savers than coat racks, because they don't consume floor space. But they do require wall space. And, they are prone to the same "spontaneously regenerative" phenomenon, growing jackets and sweaters and bags until they bulge off your wall and items slip and spill onto the floor.

Wooden carved hooks, metal hooks, decorative molding hooks, even antique hooks allow you to add a personal touch to the entryway. Some hook systems even incorporate a shelf above a series of coat pegs for entryway detritus such as keys and mail. I've even seen some with mirrors incorporated into the design, which adds even more practicality to the entry piece, but I'm skipping ahead.

If your front door is heavy enough, you may be able to attach a few decorative hooks directly onto it, giving you a place to hang a purse and sweater if you have absolutely no wall space for a hook.

By the way, hooks needn't be limited to the hallway. Kate,

twenty-nine, from Grand Rapids, Michigan, has hooks around her home in several convenient places. Her husband's guitars hang on some, her baby backpack on another. "Otherwise, these things would just lie against a wall and we'd trip over them," she says.

A Place for Shoes

If your nest has a no-shoe policy, like that of Justine, thirty-one, from Mountain View, California, you'll also want some way to organize the footwear abandoned by your doorstep. Even if your nest doesn't have such a policy, you may want to consider a similar solution for times of the year when muddy, wet soles are not allowed beyond the welcome mat.

"When you walk into our home, you see a coat rack on the wall and a shoe rack below it," Justine explains. "If it's cold, we like to offer slippers to our guests."

Leah, thirty-six, from Wichita, Kansas, has a mudroom for an entryway to her home. To limit the clutter of shoes, gardening tools, and pet paraphernalia, she keeps old wooden boxes to hold these things.

Daisy, thirty-one, from Queens, New York, came up with this solution to the shoe-clutter problem. She keeps a giant bowl in her open-arched coat closet next to her entry. In it, she and her husband throw all their shoes, from flip-flops to rollerblades, thereby eliminating them from the floor.

A Place for Keys, Mail, and Other Entryway Tidbits

Not only is it useful to have a spot to throw your keys near the door, but it's also practical, since you typically only need these when you are leaving your nest. Having them in a predetermined spot will save you hours of frustration looking for them when you're trying to leave in a hurry.

Likewise, it's helpful to have a place to store other items you usually only need when leaving the house—outgoing mail, a dog leash, cell phone, sunglasses, loose change, your wallet or purse.

If you have the space for a little receiving table with one or two drawers, these are often great for entryways—you can hide your junk in the drawers and still have a pleasing piece upon which to display books, art, flowers, or pictures—whatever you would like to be greeted with upon entering your nest.

Lana, twenty-nine, from Los Angeles, found a small wooden CD cabinet that she painted and placed just inside her front door. "If this cabinet weren't there, there'd be no Holy Place for my keys, and I'd never be able to find them," she says.

If your nest offers limited or no wall space for a table, consider this creative option: Hannah, thirty-four, from Van Nuys, California, set up several hanging baskets just inside the door for things like outgoing mail, dry cleaning, items that need to be returned—library books and videos—keys, wallets, and cell phones. Hanging baskets on the front door itself might also be an option, but since the door swings open, they should be carefully secured.

For others, there may be no other option than to designate an area to dump your stuff until you can get to it. Jessica, thirty-six, from Rome, has a spot in her kitchen, where she tosses the diaper bag and kids' coats until she has a chance to hang them up in the closet.

Jackie, thirty-two, from El Dorado, California, has two designated corners in the den—one for her, one for her husband—where both have license to leave their personal postwork items (such as laptops and breast-pumping equipment). Since they access these items both in the morning and at night, they feel fine leaving them out in the open, hiding them only when guests come over.

For those with an entry closet but no wall space, another option may be to remove the closet door altogether and turn the closet into a tiny receiving nook instead. For instance, you could remove the clothes rod and any shelving that might be inside, and replace these with a coat rack or series of hooks on the wall, along with a mirror and tiny table with drawers.

Painting the inside of this closet a complementary color to the hallway might help define the space as its own (keep it light, though, or you'll never be able to see what's inside unless there's a window in the closet).

A light in this nook is critical for such tasks as sorting mail and putting on lipstick. If your closet lacks one, consider a battery-operated light, since there probably isn't an electrical outlet inside the closet. Of course, if you use the front closet to hide all your junk or as overflow storage for your bedroom closet, this might not be an option, but hanging a mirror and basket on the inside of the door may give you a place to stash your keys and cell phone as you hang up your coat.

A Place to Primp

Maybe this is a bit girly of me to include, but I have an enormous amount of appreciation for people who have a mirror by the door-way. This perhaps stems from my days as a motorcycle maven—crossing the Bay Bridge on a windy night and entering a party with helmet hair and a nose bright red from the cold wasn't exactly the greatest first impression. It is always nice to have one last visual check before entering someone's home or heading out the door.

Wall space for a mirror is required, of course. But if you have an unused corner in the entry area, a small freestanding mirror might work. A closet door is an option, too, for hanging a cute mirror. Just be sure to get the type of mounting hooks that will prevent the mirror from swinging and bumping against the door every time you open it.

Ambiance

Practicalities aside, it's time to consider mood. I think the entryway begs for ambiance. The entry sets the tone for what's to come, giving you and your guests a first impression. It also tends to be the spot where visitors linger at the end of the night.

How to create this ambiance? Aside from indirect lighting, which I cover extensively in Chapter 8, "Lighting," consider a few extra details, space willing. A chair or small bench not only serves the practical purposes of giving you a place to comfortably take off muddy shoes, set down a bag of groceries while you de-coat, or sort through mail—but it also begs a guest to linger just a little longer when saying good-bye. A chair also serves as a symbolic reminder that rest and restoration is on the agenda when entering home. It's a pleasant greeting every time you enter the nest.

Collections or displays that reveal something about the nester inside are a charming way to decorate an entryway. Old family portraits, I adore. A series of charcoal sketches done during previous travels, *très chic*. A collection of antique colored-glass bottles on a shelf mounted above the door, quaint.

No space for any of this? Perhaps you need to think outside of the box. Or, outside of the nest, as the case may be. Lana, twenty-nine, from Los Angeles, has no entry area in her nest, but solved the problem by creating a "foyer" on the landing just in front of her apartment door. A few plants, a sculpture, a gorgeous mat, and fun French magnet signs on the door turn her landing into a "room" filled with mood and ambiance to welcome her guest.

closets

Those of you who have read my second book, *Hitched: The Go-Girl Guide to the First Year of Marriage,* already know that one of the secrets to a sexy marriage is ample closet space. I wrote that partially in jest (of course you can have a sexy marriage sans walk-in closet), but according to my research with married women, sharing a tiny closet with one's mate is not only challenging, but also a pain in the . . . well, you get the point.

Because our closets are where we dress (or plan our outfits), store our delicate silks and linens, and (typically) cram in all that other stuff we don't know what to do with—and because most of us starting out in marriage or in our first apartments can't afford the luxury of walk-in rooms to house our clothes—we have to make do with what we have. Which is usually very little. Closets, though, often contain unused space or mismanaged space consumed by clutter, and that's what this section is about.

I'm assuming, here, that you have little or no closet space to spare, because that is what I heard over and over in my surveys with women on the subject. If you are one of the lucky few who don't suffer from this problem, then skip this part or read it to sympathize with the rest of us. I write from experience: I share a closet with my husband—one rod, three feet long, in a space no deeper than our refrigerator. Trust me, it can be done.

Step One: Banish the Junk

Once a year, examine your closets and other places where you stash clothing and "stuff" and pick out the items you have not worn or used over the past year (minus the special-occasion ensembles that are rarely touched).

Of these pieces, ask yourself the following two questions: "Am I keeping this because it was expensive and even though I never wear/ use it now, there's a chance I might someday?" And: "Does this have emotional value for me?"

If you answered yes to the former question, then you need to kiss the piece good-bye—it is taking up valuable space in your closet and only reminding you of a bad purchase. Tell yourself that some lucky chick will be forever thankful to you for giving it up at a consignment store or charity. Then, place it in a giveaway pile and move on to the next item that's taking up valuable closet space.

If you answered yes to the latter question—the piece has emotional value, even though you never wear/use it—then set that aside for long-term storage. (We'll discuss this in a minute.)

"But what if I regret it later?" you ask. Listen, I have done the closet purge several times over the past decade, giving away thousands of dollars worth in fine clothing and fine "stuff" because it no longer fits (hate to break it to you, girlfriend, but the body changes over time), or because I had just stopped using it.

Truth be told, I've regretted only one giveaway—a flared chocolate-brown wool coat I sent to the Salvation Army because I was sick of it and had purchased a new one (the coat was in fine condition and perfect for between-seasons weather). Now that I've had a break from it, I miss it. But whenever I get wistful about that chocolate-brown coat, I just remind myself that some other terribly fashionable woman out there has been getting good use out of that coat for the past five years. That makes me feel better.

If there are items you're just not ready to part with as you begin to clean out the closets, put those "maybes" in a pile and wait six months. If you still haven't touched them, face it—it's time to say good-bye forever.

Amanda, twenty-seven, from Chicago, uses the "if it makes me feel frumpy, it's gone" rule to deal with her "teeennnyyy bedroom and matching closet space." That's a good one to follow, because, as Reese, twenty-nine, from Cleveland, Ohio, puts it, "I've learned that much of what you store you don't even need." Her neighborhood has two garage sales a year. Striving to be a minimalist, she stores up items she wants to give away until the next sale.

Step Two: Divide and Conquer

The next step in making more storage space is to separate the items in your "to-keep pile" into three categories: frequently used, seasonal or annual, and special occasion. I suggest taking every thing out of the closet during this step, so you can give the floor, walls, any shelving you may have, and the ceiling a good cleaning while you're at it. A fresh space helps motivate you to minimize your stuff.

The frequently used items and those that are currently in-season are the pieces that go back into your closets. Store the rest elsewhere (again, we'll talk about that in a minute). Of the frequently used clothing, decide which of these pieces are best hung and which should be folded or placed on shelves within easy reach.

Fabric care etiquette dictates that you fold most knitted items and casual wear, such as jeans, khakis, and workout clothes on shelves or in drawers. Hang the more delicate and pressed pieces from a rod.

Place the "hung" pieces back in your closet in matching lengths. For instance, all shirts should go together, all short skirts, then pants, then long skirts, then dresses and coats. Keep matching separates, like suits, together if you are like me and need that type of simplification in order to get dressed in the morning.

I am not being anal by suggesting length segregation. Doing so will free valuable floor space underneath the shorter items. There, you can place a shoe rack, freestanding shelves or a drawer system, a clothes hamper, luggage, or storage bins. Watch the clutter vanish.

Step Three: Survey the Territory

Once the frequently used pieces are back on rods and shelves or in drawers, assess the remaining space you have. Examine your closet from floor to ceiling and ask yourself if a different setup might be better for the clothing left.

For instance, a single rod at eye level wastes more usable space than two rods, one above the other, spaced about forty inches apart. This accommodates two rows of short-length items, such as shirts or pants folded over a hanger. Look at the walls above your clothing rods and assess whether a shelf could be added to store lesser-used items. Is any other wall space available? If you have a closet door, could hooks or baskets be attached there to store purses, belts, hats, or a shoe bag?

A shoe rack placed beneath the clothing on the floor gets rid of the mess of shoes. So does a canvas shelving system, hung on free space of the clothing rod. Jackie, thirty-two, from El Dorado, California, claims that the canvas shoe storage system was the best closet purchase she has ever made: "There were two outcomes," she says. "It removed the clutter of shoes from the floor, and I wear different shoes more often, because now I can see what I have."

Extra wall space in the closet could accommodate a tall, thin set of drawers or freestanding shelving to hold lingerie, stockings, linens, or nightwear. Keep in mind, shallow shelves are ideal in clos-ets for storing sweaters, bins of lingerie or socks, special-occasion shoes, and all those odds and ends that end up in the bedroom closet for lack of other storage options.

For more ideas on storage options, check out the resources sec-tion at the back of this book (page 257)—there are several Web sites that offer adaptation solutions for the never-ending problem of tiny closet space.

Step Four: Hide Remaining Treasures

If you have been following my advice thus far, you should have sev-eral piles of "stuff" containing special-occasion wear, out-of-season clothing, annual items, and those odd bits of stuff you had no idea what to do with so you crammed them into the closet (sports equip-ment, old tax files, camera supplies, ancient magazines).

If you have any leftover space in your refreshed closet, hang up the special-occasion wear next. Even though you rarely use it, you want it to be accessible when opportunity knocks. If you have a spare closet in another room, though, that might be a better place for fancy attire, so it won't begin to cram up the space you need more frequently (and so your fancy attire doesn't get all crammed up either).

Store seasonal and annual clothing pieces separately in areas that are less easy to access. Traditionally, Labor Day and Memorial Day were the seasonal clothing swap days—remember that old edict: never wear white after Labor Day. Or was it linen? Anyway, this calendar-dictated switch might still work for those of you who live in seasonally-defined regions, but this would never work for me, since northern Californian summers can be as chilly as winter in Wyoming, and winter days here may be as warm as Waikiki.

Bulky sweaters, tights, thick socks, and heavy jackets can be safely stored away in summer, as can tanks and shorts in winter. Airtight boxes or canvas bags are great for these. Some sizes are capable of sliding under the bed, but they can also be stored in the pantry or on the highest, most inaccessible shelf in your closet until needed.

As for all the other stuff—sports equipment, old tax files, photography or knitting supplies—the best spot to store these items is near the area where you most often use them. Sports and camping equipment can be stored in crates, bins, racks, buckets, or on shelves or hooks in the garage, if you have one, since typically you need these things on the way to the gym or tennis court or climbing wall or trip to the backcountry. Lola, thirty-two, from Olympia, Washington, keeps her gym clothes in bags in her closet, so she can "just grab one and go."

For some types of equipment, you'll want to use waterproof storage containers, but be sure to allow air to circulate within covered bins if the objects within need ventilation. Jackie, thirty-two, from El Dorado, California, keeps all her sports equipment in the garage in plastic baskets and milk crates on shelves. "All the balls go in one bin, hiking boots in another," she says.

If you lack a garage, find creative ways of storing this stuff inside your nest—an entryway closet would make sense, as might wall or ceiling hooks for, say, a bike near the back door. Colorful bins stacked neatly by the door might be another solution. (Bins might not be your ideal aesthetic, but they sure beat staring at spilled cans of tennis balls and tangled climbing gear when you're trying to relax on the sofa.)

The key to managing clutter is finding decorative ways to contain it all so your shelves and tabletops and empty floor space are not jammed or overflowing with stuff. Wall shelves—and lots of them—

are one way to create more storage space for these items, many of which can be carefully hidden in decorative baskets or boxes.

If your "stuff" has a decorative quality, don't be afraid to display it in a deliberate matter, rather than stack it in a corner, where it might look messy. A collection of cameras, for instance, could be left out for display on a bookshelf, while lenses, film, and other supplies are hidden in decorative wooden boxes placed on the shelf beneath.

Hannah, thirty-four, from Van Nuys, California, designed a cubby system to deal with the toy, games, and book clutter in her children's rooms. Inside the cubby-styled bookshelves, she placed several woven basket "drawers" that fit perfectly inside the cubbies to hold small plastic toys.

Baskets, by the way, seem to be the storage option of choice for toys, according to the mothers I interviewed. "We keep lots of covered wicker baskets for toys in every room," says Laura, thirty-two, from Warren, Michigan. "Most are fun and funky, look good, and perform well under serious dragging around."

Jackie, thirty-two, from El Dorado, California, also lives by the basket solution: "We keep two big, neat, woody, ruddy baskets under a table that backs into the sofa. They're perfect for throwing toys in when company comes over."

Roomie Advice

What to do with a roommate's clutter? Sally, twenty-nine, from New York City, who shares her nest with her boyfriend, keeps a basket in her boyfriend's closet where she can chuck all the things he's left around the apartment.

If your nest is large enough to accommodate a piece of furniture designated for storage, this makes for a clean, smooth solution. An old dresser holds tablecloths and linens in the front entryway of the nest of Joanna, thirty-one, from Los Angeles. She also uses an old computer cabinet with doors to hide her electronic equipment "so all that stuff and its mess disappears when we're not using it."

As you well know, many home décor and design stores offer ample storage units for media centers and workstations. Twyla, thirty-four, from Dallas, uses an armoire to hide her laptop, printer, fax, and all her office supplies in the dining room. When she's working, she spreads out documents on the dining-room table.

Chests, benches with hidden storage boxes beneath, and china cabinets are other standard furniture items worth considering for stashing excess "stuff." One of the most creative storage pieces I've seen belongs to Zoe, thirty-three, from Dallas. She found an old pie safe at an antique store (this six-foot-tall wooden piece was likely used in the early half of the century for cooling pies and storing foodstuff), and it now holds Zoe's serving platters, photographs, and other scraps of clutter in its shelves and drawers.

Another favorite furniture piece for storage I came across in interviewing belongs to Olive, twenty-eight, from Boston. She uses a vintage military locker to hold all her art supplies. Because it's deep, she can cram in a lot of stuff, and she loves it because it's old and interesting and functional.

CREATIVE STORAGE SOLUTIONS

Still having trouble figuring out how to manage the clutter? These women came up with the following creative solutions:

"I use hatboxes to store everything, from scarves to sewing supplies. It makes my bedroom look like some eccentric Aunt Mame character lives there."

—Carissa, thirty-five, from Chicago

"Vintage coffee and sugar tins hold my hair accessories, which make such a clutter when they're out and about on the dresser."

—Olive, twenty-eight, from Boston

"Clear shoe boxes that stack: one for cards and stationery, one for toiletries, one for shoe polish, one for hardware."

—Drew, thirty-three, from New Hartford, NY

"I like to buy old wooden toolboxes from flea markets and old beverage crates for storage."

—Leah, thirty-six, from Wichita, Kansas

"I vacuum-pack clothing and bedding that's out of season, like feather beds and extra-warm sweaters, in plastic bags to protect them from insects and dust."

—Alice, thirty-four, from San Diego

> "I use sturdy storage boxes for excess clothes, but cover them in sarongs from Nepal. They double as a pretty stand for my stereo."
>
> —*Magda, twenty-four, from Tiffin, Ohio*

> "I purchased a secondhand wooden spice rack with nice glass bottles to hold my vitamin and allergy pills. Seeing the pills mounted on my bathroom wall reminds me to take them each morning."
>
> —*Lana, twenty-nine, from Los Angeles*

the kitchen

Most of us lack the necessary cash to design and build a more perfect kitchen in our nest. If we did, this room might include a long wooden table, a top-of-the-line range and oven, a dishwasher, a new refrigerator with all the works, and a wood-burning stove in the corner for ambiance, since the kitchen is where guests always hang out. And, the kitchen would incorporate enough counter space to slaughter a lamb and roll out pastry dough for a rhubarb pie at the same time—on opposite sides of the room, naturally.

Alas, most of our kitchens are tiny, lack adequate surfaces for prepping food, make a mockery of storage needs, and, in the words of Zoe, thirty-three, from Dallas, "have cabinets that were built by a dyslexic, cheap, design-challenged, eight-foot-tall carpenter."

Since redoing a kitchen is a costly venture—not to mention an unrealistic one if you're a renter—we must make do with the setup we have. Luckily, several easy storage guidelines offer inexpensive ways to organize the space and tools you need to cook, if not look, like Nigella Lawson. Organizing eliminates that cluttered look that can destroy an otherwise calm space in which to prepare meals.

Pots and Pans

Cookware is best stored near the stove and oven, which is where you need pots and pans and cookie sheets. If you lack cabinets within an arm's length of the stove, affix a hanging rack to the wall or ceiling above. This is the setup I use; it not only adds charm to the kitchen, but it is also the most convenient storage I've ever had for these items.

I've also seen gorgeous cookware displays along kitchen walls—each pot or pan is mounted onto a wall near the stove. Of course, if you have copper cookware, this is an especially nice touch—that wall will glitter like sunlight. And if you need to sauté some garlic, just grab a pan from above and go.

What to do with all the lids? If you have a drawer also within arm's length of the stove, consider placing them in there. Another option is to buy a hanging rack made specifically for lids. There is nothing cozy or sensual about searching for the right lid when your spaghetti sauce is sputtering onto the walls.

Mixing Bowls, Wooden Spoons, Knives, and Chopping Boards

Stack mixing bowls on shelves near your primary food-prep spot, so they are easily accessible when you need to separate eggs or combine all the dry ingredients.

Chopping boards should also be kept on or underneath the counter area where you dice onions or quarter tomatoes. Keep carving or cutting knives within reach of this area as well.

If your counter space is too slim to accommodate a knife block holder, consider those magnetic strips that you attach to the wall. Knife blades stick right to it and take up no space at all.

Stash mixing spoons, spatulas, and other cooking utensils within arm's length of this sacred food-prep area. A drawer is one option, but since you often need to grab these when your hands are covered in pastry dough or minced garlic, placing them upright in a vase or holder is often a cleaner solution.

Dishes, Glasses, and Flatware

Store these on shelves or in counters close to the sink where you wash and dry dishes. If you are lucky enough to have a dishwasher, storing dishware above this godly apparatus is ideal for putting things away.

And on the subject of sinks, organization laws dictate that it's wise to store the items you need near the sink within easy reach. This would include salad spinners and pasta strainers, as well as kitchen cleaning materials.

Appliances

Keep in view only those you use on a regular basis: the coffeemaker and grinder, the toaster, the blender. Store the appliances you only use on occasion in less convenient spots—in those eight-foot-tall cabinets above the refrigerator, on the back shelves of the pantry, in that space beneath the stairs. For the appliances you never use— Aunt Mary's inherited Crock-Pot from 1970—consider "storing" them at Goodwill.

Trash Cans

Garbage is best kept under or near the sink. This placement will save you from having to carry the dirty kitchen-sink strainer and used coffee filters across the room when you are cleaning up. Cans with lids that open with a foot lever are great for keeping the trash bin tidy—you never have to touch the lid when your hands are covered in cookie dough.

Recycling bins can be hidden elsewhere, ideally in the pantry if you have one. However, if you have space under or near the sink for your can and bottle recycling bins, keep them close to the water source—especially if the recycling program in your area asks you to rinse these out first.

Plastic and Paper Bags

Since these clutter up the nest if left out in the open, it's best to hide them until needed. If you have drawer space, paper bags fold up fairly well inside these, but an even better solution is to buy a rack created specifically for grocery paper bag storage that can be hung on the inside of a pantry or cabinet door or wall. Also available in many home retail shops are plastic bag dispensers, but an old tissue box works just as well—stuff it with the old bags you want to reuse and set aside in the pantry (we keep ours in the same drawer that holds our paper bags). When one is needed, just pull it out like a Kleenex.

Nonperishables

If you're short on cabinet space for canned soup, sauces, and boxes of pasta, the nonperishables can be tucked away elsewhere. Isabelle, thirty-one, from Sacramento, California, stores canned and other dry goods in her laundry room, since kitchen space is so tight, while Kasey, twenty-five, from Hoboken, New Jersey, uses two pieces of furniture in her apartment to store some of the kitchen stuff she doesn't use daily.

the household files

Every nest needs a safe place to store all those important documents, records, and certificates most of us keep in random places—or worse, in stacks on our dining room tables. Everyone has a different filing system that makes sense, and unless you're losing track of where you stuck that phone bill or stashed your passport, stick with what works for you. For those who have yet to organize, here are some guidelines.

Design a System to Track Items That Need Immediate Attention

Bills, for instance. If you pay your bills online, which I highly recommend for convenience sake, you will only need a way to keep track of incoming bills that need to be paid.

Many nesters, based on my research, keep a designated "to-do" tray where most of their mail goes. When they find the time to pay their bills, they clear the tray, pay, then file away receipts in whatever "household business" filing system they've designed (see the following page for example).

It is wise to keep past utility receipts, bank and credit card statements, and check receipts for expenses such as rent for at least one year. In the event of a mix-up, you're covered.

Hannah, thirty-four, from Van Nuys, California, came up with this system to track urgent paperwork: Rather than have all her bills, articles torn out of magazines, and paint chips piled up on tabletops, she devised a color-coordinated filing system for everything. Bills go in a red folder (urgent) the kids' school papers are filed in a yellow folder (like a school bus) magazine clip-outs of garden ideas go into the green folder (get it?).

Create a "Household Business" Filing System

The "Business" files hold all those important documents that pertain to your nest and other worldly possessions. If you're just starting out, it may help to see how someone else does it. I'll expose my drawers for this purpose. Here is a sample of how I organize my files:

- Automobile (title records and maintenance receipts go in one folder, car insurance information in another)
- Computer/Office Equipment (files include users' guidelines, warranties, and Internet provider account information)
- Education (here you'll find my college degree, a copy of my transcript, and student loan payoff letters)
- Financial Accounts (separate folders keep track of my checking/savings account documents and credit card statements)
- Household (this includes folders for various utilities, as well as docs for home insurance, title, mortgage records, home improvement receipts, and property taxes)
- Investment Accounts (herein are receipts for CDs and bonds)

- Health Care (where I keep information about my PPO and past medical claims)
- Miscellaneous (for birth and marriage certificates, and other various documents)
- Retirement (files keep track of IRA and 401(k) statements and my social security card)
- Travel (herein I store my passport, upcoming travel reservations and tickets, and airline mileage statements)
- Warranties (where I stick all those household appliance instruction manuals, receipts, and warranties)
- Wills (a copy of mine, my husband's, and those of various family members)

Because I am self-employed, I store my tax return files and the current year's receipts and write-offs separately. And because that process is very involved, I'll spare you the details. In uncomplicated tax matters, a separate file marked TAXES might contain pay stub receipts, copies of W-4s and W-2s, and any other relevant tax information that gathers dust over a tax year. Past tax returns should be kept for at least seven years in the event you are audited. I store these in a box under the stairs, since I hopefully will never have to access them!

Note: Financial experts advise that you store many of the items I've mentioned above—car titles, birth certificates, passports—in a safety-deposit box in a secured location. At a minimum, keep these files locked and in a fireproof filing cabinet if they reside in your nest.

Establish an "Inspiration File" for Your Nest

Gretchen, thirty-two, from St. Paul, Minnesota, keeps a file of clever ideas she comes across in home décor magazines. Whenever she plans a trip to a flea market, she browses through her files and makes a list of things to look for.

I also keep a "Home Renovation" file in a separate drawer from my business files. Herein, I drop ads I've clipped out of the paper for

ORGANIZE YOUR ADDRESSES

So you never lose touch, keep track of addresses in two places:

1. Your computer: There are many programs that will organize your addresses for you, making it easy to print out a guest list and labels when you're planning a party or sending out a fund-raising letter. With addresses, emails, and phone numbers saved on your hard drive, backed up whenever your friends move (which is all the time, don't you think?), you'll never risk "losing" your address book on the bus.

2. Portable address keeper: Whether it's a Palm Pilot, standard Rolodex, or a delicate address book covered in parchment, you'll want to tote your collection of addresses with you when traveling. Update addresses whenever you update them on your computer and you'll always be current. Keep your portable at home by the phone unless you're out and about (so you don't have to turn on the laptop every time you want to make a phone call).

furniture items I want, gardening designs and tips, paint colors I like, and do-it-yourself techniques for such jobs as refinishing furniture. Whenever my husband and I decide to tackle our next "project," I flip through my folder to see if I came across some brilliant idea for said project that I have entirely forgotten about since I filed it away. This folder is also great for tossing in business cards of antique or home furnishing stores I like or any other nesting inspiration I want to give a try when I find the time.

the photographs

The final frontier in organizing your nest involves the images of our past that most of us keep buried in shoeboxes under our beds. Digital cameras have made the whole mess much easier to deal with—no negatives you must store, no blurry, bad prints you can't bear to throw out for reasons quite unknown. And with digital, you can only print the images you want to keep, knowing that the not-so-great images are safely stored on your hard drive or a CD should you ever wish to access them.

Still, most of us also have a pile or two of ancient photographs in a bag or shoebox in the back of the closet that we just don't want to deal with. If you're like me, those old photos are cluttering up valuable space. Organizing them could not only free up more room for shoes, but also give you peace of mind that the evidence of your twenty-first birthday celebration will never fade away in those bags.

The first step in organizing old photos is to drag them all out into the light and see what you've got. My advice is to take them out in chunks—if they are still in envelopes from the developer, work one roll at a time.

Spread them out on your bed or floor, then pull out the images that create some sort of emotional draw—it's beautiful, historical, funny, even nostalgic. Be sure to include a mix of people, landscapes, buildings, events—images that remind you of a past moment that has meaning to you.

Put these pictures aside, then examine all the rest, asking yourself if you really need to keep all those blurry images of your first pet snake (surely you preserved a better image of Cleo elsewhere). If you have no clue at what you're looking at in some of these pictures, place that image in a reject pile. If you can't remember now, you definitely won't remember when you're eighty.

For those of you ready to kiss clutter good-bye forever, throw all the rejects away. I know that sounds utterly heartless and cruel, but you will enjoy the good images *even more* if they aren't contaminated by the bad ones, too. (For those sentimentalists who can't bear the thought of tossing away a bad photograph, do me a favor and put these aside anyway for now—after you've whittled down the images you really do love and placed them in an album, you may feel differently about it.)

If you plan to store these images in chronological order (my recommendation for general organizational purposes), place the good ones back in the envelope you found them, along with their negatives, then move on to the next stack. Do this until all your old photos, good and bad, have been refreshed in your memory. Warning: This is a multiple-day, if not -week, event, so be sure to spread out this project in a safe area so your images won't get trampled on in the meantime.

The next step is to decide how you want to store the keepers. If space really is the issue here, you may want to go with the acid-free, lignin-free, PVC-free photo archival albums—the type that enable you to jot down notes and dates alongside the image, using acid-free ink. (Acid, lignin, and the polyvinyl chloride in some plastic sleeves, by the way, can damage photographs over time.) Buy several of these albums so you don't have to keep making trips to the camera store. You will use up any extras in years to come.

Placing images chronologically is arguably the easiest way to store them and the most accessible in terms of viewing. The notes will always remind you what year and event you're looking at. In these albums, do not include those uninspiring images you separated from the ones you liked. Those can also go wherever you're storing the negatives, or better, in the trash can.

Keep all the corresponding negatives in a protected envelope tucked into the back of the book or stored separately in archival acid-free sleeves or boxes (be sure to indicate which grouping of negatives correspond to which photo album). To be utterly safe, store negatives in a fireproof filing cabinet or safe.

Jennifer, thirty-two, from Concord, Georgia, has her husband store all their negatives at his office in case their photo albums are destroyed in a fire. Also, keep all albums and negatives in a dark, dry room with low humidity (not in the kitchen or bathroom or sauna!).

Another storage option for the photos you want to keep and access often is in photographic archival boxes. Justine, thirty-one, from Mountain View, California, recently revamped her storage system using this method. She cleared out her photo-holding shoeboxes and placed the pics in chronological order in archival binder boxes, labeled clearly on the outside. "It's almost too organized," she says. "It takes very little time to find photos I'm looking for."

The key to keeping on top of photos is to file them away as soon as you get them. That way they won't begin to pile up. Magda, twenty-four, from Tiffin, Ohio, keeps on hand pretty blank photo books and photo corners (which are those little triangular photo holders that stick onto a page in an album and enable you to safely secure the photo without using damaging scotch tape or glue).

Whenever she gets a roll back, she puts the pictures in a book and immediately labels them. "People like looking through organized, labeled pictures," she says. "They tell a story better than a random pile."

Jackie, thirty-two, from El Dorado, California, who has gone digital, purchased ten albums for future use, which eliminated the decision of what type of album to get the next time she was ready to store pictures.

To keep track of her digital pics, she uses a binder to hold two things: CDs with digital images and a matching index page. On that page, she makes notes about the event photographed or other details, like her daughter's age. She only prints the images she really loves, and places those in real albums to show off to others.

NESTING PLEASURES:
DESIGN A SCRAPBOOK

Perfect for presenting pictures that follow a certain theme, these contemplated albums go beyond chronological events. They make great gifts: "Jeanie's Bachelorette Days," for instance, might chronicle pics of the premarriage years for a girlfriend about to tie the knot. Themed albums are also great for preserving photos, say, of a recent trip to New Zealand, that you know you'll be pulling out and showing off to friends and family.

Next rainy day, flip through your stacks of photos (or flip through your albums) and pull out images that might combine to make a stunning, entertaining scrapbook perfect for your nest.

Materials:
Photographs and/or memorabilia
Archival-quality album
* Acid-free or Mylar mounting corners or archival-quality mounting squares or adhesive
* Archival paper for labels and acid-free glue for attaching labels (album permitting)
* Acid-free ink pens

1. Decide what type of album you'd like to make. There are no rules here. Let the images you have guide you. Flip through any chronologically organized albums you own for

inspiration, then pull out the pictures that call upon a certain theme.

Do you have millions of images of ex-boyfriends that you have no idea what to do with now that you've found The One? Make an "Ex-Boyfriend Album." Then when you're done, burn it! (Or not.)

Stymied on what to do with all those college and post-college party pics? Make an album entitled: "My Twenty-Something Years." If you're still in your twenties, be sure to leave room for what's to come. You can end this book, of course, with pics from your thirtieth birthday bash.

If you're the type to take photos of interesting buildings and art while traveling, create an album solely dedicated to architecture or art, noting the date, city, and/or museum in which you snapped the shot. Voila! Your own personalized art book.

2. Choose the right album. If you're the type who likes to include memorabilia—concert tickets, menus, brochures, dried flowers preserved in Ziploc bags, a watercolor you painted when you were in Rome—along with photographs, be sure to choose an album that accommodates the mishmash of collectibles you will preserve inside.

Also, pick an album with binding that expands due to the added bulk. Blank archival albums with expandable binders are your best bet. This also suits scrapbooks designed with pictures of varied dimensions.

3. Think composition. A good scrapbook is one that gives you pleasure every time you look at it, which typically means that it was well planned, page by page.

Before you begin with the adhesive, lay out all the images and items you wish to include. Then, look for unique ways to group the images—by subject, person, date, etc. An art album, for instance, could be arranged by museums, by images of the same artist, or by genre—Impressionism, abstract, Renaissance realism. Labels can always indicate the exact date and location an image was shot.

In general, you'll want all the images to face the same way on one page. But feel free to have some pages designed horizontally and others vertically—flipping the scrapbook to the side is only annoying if you must do so to view each image on every page.

If you are exceptionally talented with words, by all means, write something meaningful next to these images—a poem that reminds you of a certain picture, a quote pertaining to a place or statue of a person whose image you snapped, an abstract from your journal, written around the time you took the picture.

4

Tidying the Twigs

The Blue Tit of Corsica weaves aromatic herbs into its nest to ward off bacteria and parasites.

 Before we get to the fun part of decorating the nest, there is one more matter worth discussing on the topic of composing your nest—cleaning.

Unscientific as my observations may be, the homes of true nesters are tidy, fresh, and lack obvious dirt and grime. For this reason, my own nest would not qualify as "nesty" about half of the time. I'm working on it.

By clean, I do not mean the nest smells of ammonia or fake pine needles the moment you walk in the door. I simply mean that there are no day-old dishes haunting the sink, no ancient spiderwebs capitalizing ceiling corners, no dust bunnies multiplying before your eyes, no globs of toothpaste contaminating the bathroom sink or splattered across the medicine cabinet mirror.

Instead, the floors are clean, critical surfaces shine (we'll discuss which ones in a minute), and the air smells like air, not mold or must.

These cozy homes are not only clean but are also tidy. Yesterday's newspaper does not spill off the living-room coffee table. Shoes are not strewn haphazardly about the house. And the bed looks so freshly made, you want to dive right into the sheets and roll around when no one is looking.

A clean and tidy nest is a place where the senses may open up and relax. It is a haven, where a nester can rejuvenate from the battles of city living or suburban blues. In a clean kitchen, one is more likely to cook sensual meals. In a clean bathroom, one is assured instant home-spa escapism when emergencies call for it.

Fresh sheets promote fresh dreams after an anxiety-provoking day. And the best thing about keeping the nest freshly aired is that it doesn't cost a cent (aside from the few cleaning supplies you will need to keep on hand). For those who are very short on cash to pad the nest, it's amazing what tidiness can do.

a definition of clean, please

In my interviews with other nesters, I found a wide range of opinions on what constitutes a clean nest. In general, visible dirt, dust, or grime seemed to be the universal sign that a cleaning is due.

How often must we break out the dustpan? Some nesters do a full cleaning, consisting of dusting, mopping, vacuuming/sweeping, and scrubbing the bathroom and kitchen, once a week. Others stretch the chore out to once a month. But the average time between inspirations, I found, was every two weeks.

Many nesters also engage in seasonal or annual cleanings to

tackle all sorts of tasks—polishing the silver inherited from Aunt Eunice, airing out the rugs, and dry-cleaning the down feather comforter.

Motivation, or lack of, as the case may be, is often the biggest deterrent to regular cleaning, perhaps second only to lack of leisure time (who wants to spend a sunny Saturday afternoon with Clorox?). But I've also found that a lack of know-how on cleaning efficiently also contributes to the procrastination.

What type of products do you use? And what's the most efficient way to clean? What areas should you concentrate on if you only have fifteen minutes to spot clean before a hot date shows up for a home-cooked dinner (a suggestion you made after two martinis and several culinary-type innuendoes)?

This chapter offers answers to the most basic cleaning techniques and strategies for busy birds who don't want to spend all their free time with a mop in hand. If you're a pro on the subject, go ahead and skip this chapter. But the next time you feel unmotivated to clean, flip through the next dozen pages or so and see if they don't give you the boost of inspiration you need to tidy up your twigs.

"where do i begin?"

If you are short on time for cleaning, which I'm assuming you are, you really only need to concentrate on a few universal magnets of filth in the nest in order to psyche yourself (and others) into believing that you're living in a clean nest. These areas are as follows, in no particular order.

Kitchen Sink and Stove

Since the sink and stove are usually composed of surfaces that are meant to shine, such as metal, tile, or porcelain, a nest will look and smell clean if you make a point to always keep them free of dirty dishes, pans, and bits of food.

That means doing dishes immediately after using them, then taking a sponge and wiping down these areas with soapy dishwashing water. This will keep the surfaces shiny between official cleanings, during which you can really work on that glistening finish and disinfect the area using the appropriate cleaning products.

While you're at it, spot-check the wall behind the stove and wipe away any splashes of tomato sauce or sautéed garlic that might have leapt from the pan onto the wall while you were cooking.

Focusing on these key surfaces in the kitchen will divert attention away from the bread crumbs on the butcher-block table if you're in a pinch for time before your coworker drops by for a visit.

Bathroom Sink and Toilet

These items, too, are made of materials that typically shine and therefore stand out as fresh and clean if they sparkle. Keeping a sponge, a spray bottle of all-purpose cleaner, and a squirt bottle of toilet-bowl cleaner in the bathroom will make it easy to spot clean that glob of toothpaste hardening in the sink or that something quite worse stuck to the inside of the toilet bowl.

Save the tub or shower for more intense cleaning, unless you're expecting an overnight guest, at which point a spritz of all-purpose cleaner across the tiles and floor will eliminate the most obvious of soap scum violations and shaving remnants.

Floors

A quick sweep or vacuum or Swiffer in the rooms most prone to filth accumulation—the front entryway, the dining area, the kitchen, and the bathroom—keeps the floors of your nest free of obvious dirt and dust.

If you have hardwood floors, you'll need to upkeep more often (and more carefully). Wooden floors, especially those with a semi-gloss finish, really show dirt, dust, or a melange of footprints.

Windows and Mirrors

Because our eyes naturally wander to windows and mirrors, keeping these surfaces free of handprints and smears is another way to fake cleanliness, not to mention distract from the fact that we haven't dusted the baseboards in over five months.

Linens

There are two types of linens on which to concentrate your efforts: your towels and your bedding. Newly laundered hand towels in the kitchen and bathroom always gives a fresh impression. The last thing you want to do when you go over to someone's house is wipe your squeaky clean hands on a dingy rag that is slightly damp and wadded up on the counter. Let "dry and fluffy" be your mantra.

Bed linens are important to mention because there is nothing more sensual than falling asleep atop freshly laundered sheets that smell like the very fibers from which they are composed. A weekly change of linens is critical for proper nesting in the bedroom. Between washings, fluff up your pillows each morning and throw back the covers to let your bed air out while you take a shower or walk the dog. Then, smooth the sheets before making the bed. It's amazing what this simple ritual each morning can do for the soul on a hard day's night.

The Air

The air inside your nest needs attention, too. Opening several windows throughout your home in the mornings or early evenings will help exchange stale air for new oxygen, creating an overall sense of freshness inside your nest.

Aromatheraputic candles and fresh flowers are only sensual additions if they are scenting fresh air, not trying to disguise the waft of burnt salmon drifting from the broiler or the stench of mildew coming from God knows where.

If your nest lacks windows that open, consider opening the door and using a fan to circulate the old air out and get the new air in on a regular basis. Keeping doors and windows open while you clean is a good idea, by the way. Doing so will prevent your nest from smelling like an Ajax factory when you're done.

ON GETTING DOWN AND DIRTY

Inspiration to clean often comes in surprising ways:

"Sometimes I put on loud punk music, which gets me moving."

—*Carissa, thirty-five, from Chicago*

"Planning a shindig is the only way I can motivate myself to go whole hog in the cleaning."

—*Jeanette, twenty-eight, from Castro Valley, California*

"I save fun installing or decorating tasks to do until after I clean, which makes cleaning fun."

—*Ethel, thirty-nine, from Philadelphia*

"My daughter motivates me—the sight of her dirty hands makes me cringe."

—*Isabelle, thirty-one, from Sacramento, California*

"I get motivated to clean after going over to someone else's *really* clean house."

—*Meryl, twenty-nine, from Oakland, California*

"When I see dust bunnies gathering in the hall."

—*Zoe, thirty-three, from Dallas*

"I remind myself how good I feel when the cleaning is done and think about that energized feeling that a clean house induces."

—*Reese, twenty-nine, from Cleveland, Ohio*

"I'll lure a friend over with wine to sit and talk to me while I clean. I don't ask for help, I just want company to make it go more quickly."

—*Molly, thirty-two, from San Francisco, California*

the tools

In a pinch, most cleaning can be managed with just an old rag and a spritz of all-purpose cleaner. But having the right tools makes it easier to keep the nest tidy and fresh. What follows is a rundown of the most useful tools to help nesters keep their homes neat, fresh, and sensual.

A Cleaning Carrier

For lack of a better word, a "carrier" is a tray or box with handle (a critical detail) into which you store your cleaning supplies and products. A carrier will save you from having to find, then carry, all of your cleaning rags, sponges, and potions from one room to another, spilling and dropping items along the way.

The carrier may be an old toolbox, a plastic tool tote, available at most hardware stores, or even a sturdy cardboard six-pack for those with minimalist supplies. Just make sure the sides of this carrier are tall enough to support bottles—if you get a carrier with short sides, the bottles tend to spill over and fall out unless they are perfectly balanced therein.

If you have the space in your nest and want to get decorative about it, an alternative to the cleaning carrier would be a child's toy wagon with handle or an even more space-consuming decorative wheelbarrow. You could even fashion your own model using a crate affixed to a skateboard . . . but let's not get carried away.

For those with nests so tiny even a small tool tote is a misguided use of space, consider an apron with large pockets or even a tool belt into which you can stuff several rags, hang a feather duster, and stash a bottle of multipurpose cleaner. When you're done, just hang the whole shebang, cleaning products and all, onto a hook inside a closet door.

A Bunch of Rags

You will need several old rags for dusting dry surface tops. If your cleaning regimen includes waxing or polishing wooden tabletops, you'll need rags for these, too. If you use rags instead of a feather duster, stock up with a store-bought bag or make your own from old T-shirts and sheets—the lint-free type or you'll add more dust than what you remove.

Speaking of dusters, ostrich feather dusters are one of my favorite cleaning inventions, because they work so efficiently at making dust stick to them rather than become airborne when you swipe your furniture. Not to mention they are more fun to use than a rag. Besides, every nest needs feathers! So if you have the means to purchase one, go for the gold (a real ostrich feather variety) rather than the cheap Technicolor synthetic version, which only displaces dust.

Sponges

Buy the type with an abrasive back and use them for cleaning wet surface areas, such as the kitchen countertops, the stove, the bathtub and sink. Look on the packaging for heft—if you're cleaning porcelain, tile, or stainless-steel surfaces, you'll want a mild abrasive-backed sponge to avoid scratching or dulling the surfaces.

Keep the one you use for your toilet seat separate from the others in a plastic bag clearly labeled "toilet." This will prevent you (or a well-meaning loved one) from cleaning the toilet lid and then wiping down the kitchen sink faucet. If you have roommates or live with your lover, it always helps to spell these things out to avoid any confusion on the matter.

Scrub Brushes

You'll, of course, want a toilet brush, which should be kept in the bathroom, not your carrier. If you have a porcelain toilet bowl, be sure the bristles are made of soft plastic or use the sponge version. Wire scrubbers may scruff up the surface, leaving scratch marks that look as though you tried to drown your cat.

You may also wish to buy a handheld scrub brush for kitchen and bathroom tile grout, which often needs more elbow grease. Old toothbrushes are perfect for getting grime out of little cracks and crevices in tile and around the sink faucets that larger brushes can't reach.

Floor Cleaner

If you have hardwood floors, you'll want a broom or a vacuum to keep on top of all the dust bunnies that accumulate. In my experience, vacuuming is the way to go—whenever I sweep it feels as though I'm just pushing the dirt and dust around rather than actually getting rid of it.

But if your budget or space only allows for a broom and dustpan, then try the broom with synthetic bristles. While it's not quite as romantic as the old-fashioned straw version, it tends to work better at collecting all the muck that accumulates on the floor.

Swiffers make another fine choice for hard-surface floors. Those little wipes act like a magnet for dust, making the whole job simple and quick.

Rubber Gloves

A must-wear item to protect your hands from nasty but necessary chemical cleaners.

Cleaning Products

You don't need a million and one products to freshen up your nest. The following will do the trick for basic weekly cleanings:

- one all-purpose antibacterial cleaner for the kitchen and bathroom counters, painted surfaces, and anything stainless steel or plastic
- window cleaner
- toilet bowl disinfectant (a generic abrasive cleaner will remove some of the buildup and rust, but a product made specifically for the toilet bowl does a much more thorough and sanitary job)
- tile or linoleum cleaner for kitchen and bathroom floors
- liquid abrasive cleaner for grime in sinks and tubs that your all-purpose cleaner can't conquer
- mildew remover (if your bath or shower needs it)
- oven cleaner
- carpet stain remover or, for hardwood floors, a product made specifically for cleaning and preserving wooden floors

"I love reusing things, so the thought of cleaning with something I would normally have thrown away motivates me. I use tissue paper that you get from clothing boutiques instead of paper towels to clean mirrors and windows. I use old toothbrushes for sinks and old socks for polishing shoes."

—*Olivia, thirty-one, from Berkeley, California*

NESTING PLEASURES: DESIGNATE A DOMESTIC DAY

Next dreary weekend forecast, tackle all those tasks you've been putting off. Here's how:

Materials:
Box or basket into which you can throw all the little "need to be fixed" items: loose buttons pinned to their shirts, shoes that need polish, a broken frame that needs regluing
Appropriate supplies to do the above-mentioned tasks
Your favorite cake or bread recipe
CDs you're dying to hear and DVDs or videos you're dying to see

1. Begin the day with something fun, away from your nest and preferably outdoors—a morning workout, coffee with a

girlfriend, a walk or bike ride. Getting some fresh air and a social exchange will reduce the resentment that might otherwise surface around noon if you've been doing nest repair all morning long.

2. Assess your basket of goods that need addressing for the day. Decide which ones are realistic to accomplish, and begin with the items that seem most fun.

3. If any of these tasks are manageable while watching old *Sex and the City* episodes on DVD or listening to your favorite CDs (preferably music with a kick), combine the two. Olivia, thirty-one, of Berkeley, California, designates a silver-cleaning day once a year. On a Saturday morning, she'll pull out old T-shirts and sit in front of the TV watching cooking shows while shining her silver.

4. Bake a cake between chores (but only if baking is a fun stress relief for you). Pound cakes are easy and take over an hour to bake—perfect time to, say, tackle all that ironing you've been putting off. A loaf of bread requires a good three hours with intermittent sessions of kneading, which can be quite cathartic. At the end of the day, you'll have a freshly baked good to reward yourself. Call a friend or neighbor over for a bite if you're dying for some company. Schedule this date ahead of time so you'll have something to look forward to.

getting into the habit

There are some who contend that cleaning is good for the soul. Maybe some souls benefit with a weekly inhalation of Windex, but I'm not going to lie to you, sister: Sometimes, cleaning is nothing but a chore. That's why we procrastinate on this nasty but necessary nesting ritual.

If you need help getting into the swing of cleaning, consider the following effective tactics.

Effective Tactic One: Make a Schedule

I know it sounds anal and unliberating to tell yourself that you will clean your nest every second Wednesday night (or whenever), but establishing a rule will ensure that weeks don't pass before you begrudgingly pull out your cleaning carrier. I say begrudgingly because you've waited so long between cleanings that the dust and grime are worse than ever and, thus, far more discouraging to tackle. Taking a systematic approach to tidying the twigs makes the whole process less overwhelming.

The first step is to decide what needs to be done and how often.

Daily Cleaning Tasks
These commonly include the dishes, bed making, clothes hanging, and general de-cluttering.

Weekly or Bi-Weekly Chores
Depending on your preference, these often include kitchen and bathroom cleaning, doing the laundry, dusting, and giving the floors a once-over with a broom, vacuum, or mop.

Monthly Tasks
These may involve swiping down the cobwebs in corners and the dust on the baseboards, airing out the sofa cushions, and dusting off the window coverings and sills.

Seasonal Chores

For those who have seasonal urges to really air out the nest, make time for such chores as cleaning under and behind all the furniture, washing windows, scouring the oven and fridge, and polishing the silver you inherited from your great-grandmother.

Establishing a cleaning day for the weekly or bi-weekly cleanings can help ensure the job gets done. Brice, twenty-six, from Chicago, normally cleans on Sunday, "because that's when all my clothes are sprawled over the place and, possibly, I had guests over for drinks and apps the night before."

Magda, twenty-four, from Tiffin, Ohio, cleans on Fridays after work if she has the energy. "Then I'm more comfortable for the rest of the weekend," she says. Maria, thirty, from Brooklyn, New York, also prefers Friday as a cleaning day and got into the habit of cleaning after work—until her husband couldn't take it anymore and hired a cleaning person. "He'd want to go to dinner on Friday night, and he'd walk in the door with me on my hands and knees cleaning the grout in the tiles in the bathroom," she says.

If establishing a Holy Cleaning Day is too fundamental for your lifestyle, there are unorthodox times to tidy your nest. Meryl, twenty-nine, from Oakland, California, for instance, has been known to get motivated around midnight. "Late at night, I'll get a second wind and vacuum. Or, sometimes, I'll do unusual tasks, like clean all the doorjambs."

Hannah, thirty-four, from Van Nuys, California, squeezes in a task whenever she can grab a few minutes: "I'll dust the living room while I'm watching TV, wipe down the kitchen counters while I'm waiting for bread to toast, or scrub out the bathtub during a long Saturday morning shower."

Effective Tactic Two: Put the Process in Writing

If you are the type to get completely overwhelmed before tackling the dust on your weekly or bi-weekly cleaning, write down all the tasks you wish to accomplish and in what order, on an index card: dust apartment; wipe down kitchen counters, stovetop, sink, and windows; sweep all floors, etc. Keep this list tucked into your cleaning carrier so you don't have to think or plan every time you reach for the all-purpose cleaner—you simply follow orders on the cards.

You might also consider writing down the estimated amount of time each activity requires, so you can plan your cleaning accordingly. This works particularly well if you're not always able to clean your whole nest in one swoop.

If dusting the apartment takes fifteen minutes, which is all you have to spare before, say, a haircut appointment, you can at least get that task out of the way on a Saturday morning.

 Roomie Advice

Got kids? Laura, thirty-two, from Warren, Michigan, keeps a chore jar for her pint-sized roomies. "During a family meeting, the kids made suggestions of how they could help around the house, and we put them in a jar. Every Saturday morning, they pick out two chores and we race around the house to see who can get done the fastest. This keeps the tasks in rotation and makes it easy to delegate."

Effective Tactic Three: Make It a Ritual

Approach cleaning not as "cleaning", but as cleansing. Ritualize the process by completing each task in a predetermined order and style. That's what cleaning professionals do, and they should know how to motivate, no?

Typically, the pros will work one room at a time, tackling the dust, dirt, and grime in the following systematic way: Start with the ceilings, dusting away cobwebs, then work your way down the walls to the floors in a counterclockwise fashion around the room.

When you get to horizontal surfaces, such as tabletops and counters, clean from back to front, brushing crumbs and dust to the floor, which is always swept or vacuumed up at the end. Typically, the pros tackle the dry areas first (the windowsills and tabletops), then wipe down the wetter areas, such as sinks, windows, and last but not least, any floors that need mopping.

If this approach seems completely anal, just ignore it completely, and clean to suit your more organic personality. Carissa, thirty-five, from Chicago, uses this unique system: She gives herself a number, say thirty, and won't stop cleaning or folding laundry or putting stuff away until she's done thirty tasks or, for example, rolled up thirty pairs of socks.

Drew, thirty-three, from New Hartford, New York, gives herself a time limit before cleaning. She'll tell herself that she'll clean for X minutes. Once she reaches her goal, she stops, which prevents her from getting fed up and resentful.

Angela, thirty-four, from Houston, keeps a chart of her more intensive cleaning jobs, detailing what she'd like to get done once a month, once a quarter, etc. Whenever she grabs a moment to clean, she'll pick a task to fit that time. For instance, if she has thirty minutes to spare, she'll clean the insides of her fridge, microwave, and toaster oven.

"I NEED HELP!"

You are not alone. Some of the women I interviewed said that hiring a cleaning service once a week or every two weeks practically saved their marriages, because it eliminated all the "It's your turn to clean!" and the "I do more around the house than you do!" arguments. Many of those with roommates agreed that a professional cleaning now and then made their nests far more peaceful and fresh.

"Hiring a cleaning person to come in every so often is especially worth it if you have roommates," says Abby, twenty-six, from Woodbury, Connecticut. "It eliminates a lot of tension, because everyone has different tolerances."

Adds Leida, twenty-seven, from Seattle, "Cleaning help was the perfect solution for me and my husband—especially when we are both working full time. It has eliminated many petty arguments."

Going the professional route isn't the only option. Lana, twenty-nine, from Los Angeles, hires a high school student to do the vacuuming and bathroom cleaning twice a month. She says it's well worth the fifteen dollars per session.

If you decide to give help a try, consider the tactic used by Olivia, thirty-one, from Berkeley, California. Every six months or so, she has a crazed cleaning weekend, and sometimes employs someone to clean with her.

"You get what you want and you're there to answer any questions they may have," she says. "Even if you hire someone to come on a regular basis, my experience is that it's best to clean with them the first two times so they understand your expectations."

part two

Feathering the Nest

A Fresh Coat of Paint

The Black-chinned hummingbird uses plant down in various shades of yellow and gray to construct its colorful nest.

 Because the color of the walls is the most dominant decorative feature of a room, picking the right color, and in some cases the right texture, is critical when composing a nest to stimulate or soothe your senses, depending on what you're after. Not only does color influence the mood, but it also brings with it certain associations that recall past experiences. Cool blues and greens of the ocean may lighten your thoughts and bring on a sense of serenity, much like you'd feel on vacation at the beach. Deep reds and golds, on the other hand, may inspire a contemplative mood, such as you might experience when watching a sunset.

Adding a fresh coat of paint exposes part of yourself, too, since the hues you choose for your nest (assuming you're going with your gut preferences) reveal what you find most sensual—boldness, subtlety, warmth, cool calm. That's why debates among roommates and cohabitants often become so passionate when it comes to deciding which shade of violet is The One. That's also why picking colors, even when you live alone, can be such a daunting task—after all, it's very difficult to narrow down your sensual preferences when you're faced with so many colorful options.

Truth is, the quickest, most inexpensive—not to mention most effective—way to revolutionize your décor is to give your nest a fresh coat of paint. Getting rid of those black skid marks where the back of your favorite chair always bumps into the wall, the nicks you gouged along the doorframes when you moved all your furniture in, and the odd pockmarks created by previous art installation attempts will not only make your nest glow, but will also make your home more personalized—especially if you're the type who's not intimidated by color on the walls. Hopefully after reading this chapter you'll be eager to explore beyond the tans, whites, and beiges.

I can already hear half of you reading this book mutter the following: "But my landlord won't let me paint!" I realize the no-paint mandate is a common clause on rentals, but I also know plenty of women who've ignored that clause and painted anyway. Upon moving out, their landlords typically have said nothing—after all, they got a free paint job by looking the other way. Some city rental laws require landlords to paint a rental after a change in occupant if that occupant lived in the place for more than two years. If that's the case where you live, and if you plan on nesting at your current place for a while, then your argument (or rationale) could be that it doesn't matter what you do to the walls, short of screw up the plaster, because per rental code laws, they will have to be repainted anyway when you move out.

Sometimes landlords will let you paint even if there's a no-paint policy on the lease—as long as the colors are preapproved by him or her (and you've had good rapport with management so far). If you're lucky, your landlord might even chip in for the paint, or let you deduct the expenses from your next rent check, since you will be covering the labor—a bargain deal for both of you. But such examples of landlord generosity are rare, so don't hold me to this.

If the idea of painting overwhelms you, just sit back and relax—this chapter will give you tips on everything from choosing colors that appeal to your unique sensibility to the practicalities of prepping the room for paint.

nesting in color

Picking a paint color can be a nerve-wracking experience, especially if you consider yourself color challenged or have never had the pleasure of introducing color into your nest before. Just walking into a paint store can be an overwhelming experience—there are so many gorgeous choices! Where does a girl begin?

Start by asking yourself what colors are currently in your home or apartment's furnishings. Then, what colors do you like to wear? These are questions San Francisco interior designer Jennifer Puhalla advises her clients to consider when choosing colors for their homes. Once you know what hues you're drawn to, then you can apply color theory concepts, which will tell you what to do with those colors, she says. Of course, there are other considerations—the amount of natural light the room gets, your climate, even the style of your home. Don't worry, I'll break these down for you so by the time you've finished reading this chapter, you'll have confidence the moment you walk into a paint store.

the colors you like

Since this is the advisable place to start, take a look around your nest and closets for colors that dominate. These are likely the hues you are drawn to. If the colors that dominate are ones that you can't change and don't like—the carpeting in a rental, for instance—you'll have to work with what you've got and choose colors you like that don't clash with that.

If ugly carpeting isn't an issue, ask yourself what the colors you see around you have in common—pinks, rusts, and purples, for instance, all have red undertones. Cool blues and greens are the colors of the sea. Then, ask yourself if these colors are bold and intense or subtle pastels? The goal is to not only find recurring colors, but also patterns in your color preferences, which will give you a sense of what colors you're naturally drawn to and appeal to your sensibilities.

Another way to get inspiration for colors is by looking through design magazines and home-decorating picture books. "If I come across a color I like in a magazine, on a napkin, advertisement, or whatever, I cut it out, think about what room it might work in, and keep it in a file," says Gretchen, thirty-two, from St. Paul, Minnesota.

Leah, thirty-six, from Wichita, Kansas, who looks at magazines for inspiration, has also picked colors from fabrics that are already in the room. She finds a paint chip to match the color, then considers that for a while before purchasing paint.

If you are still at a loss, consider going to a museum—or just opening an art book. Make a mental note of the colors used in the paintings you are drawn to. (If you go the museum route, try to buy postcard versions of your favorite paintings in the gift shop, so you can take these with you to the paint store.) This has two effects. One, it will give you a sense of the colors you like as well as their intensities—are you drawn to pastel impressionists or bold abstracts? And two, these paintings will give you an automatic palette of color combinations to borrow from, because in each painting, the artist has already done the work of selecting pleasing color combinations for you.

If a museum isn't in your neighborhood, a fabric or rug store can provide the same sort of inspiration. The artists of these textiles offer automatic color combinations in their designs. If one appeals to you, note the colors and their proportions within the design, as well as the intensities of colors so you can apply a similar color scheme to your nest. Reese, twenty-nine, from Cleveland, Ohio, for instance, used a favorite rug in her dining room to inspire the colors in her house—eggplant, green, gold, and wine.

One pattern to look for is whether you're attracted to warm or cool colors. Warm colors are those that you typically see in a fire or Texan sunset—reds, oranges, golds, and pinks. Cool colors are those you might find in the ocean or the sky at dawn—blues, greens, lavenders. In a design sense, warm colors tend to evoke cozy sensations; cool colors tend to give an airy, light mood to a room. These cooler colors often work well in small spaces, too, because cool colors tend to open up the walls and give a feeling of spaciousness. They also create a calm, serene mood, which is why many designers suggest these hues for the bedroom or bath.

Warm tones, on the other hand, have the reputation of making a room feel cozier, warmer, more inviting (arguably), and in my opinion, for what it's worth, more natural—especially in nests filled with exposed wood. For these reasons, designers often steer clients toward warm hues in spaces meant for entertaining or contemplation—the living room or dining room, a study.

Mixing warm with cool tones can create an invigorating effect if it's done carefully—choosing one "temperature" as the dominate color of a room, then accenting with a hue from the opposite degree. My bedroom, for instance, has a rich adobe red on all four walls, but I've used blue-green as an accent color in a few key places, and it yields a nice balance between warm and cool.

SUCCESS STORIES (AND THEN SOME)

"My extremely macho Army-captain cousin was visiting while my husband and I were choosing paint colors for the bathroom. My cousin, oddly enough, pushed us toward a very rosy hue. While I love it, my husband calls it the 'Paris bordello bathroom.'"

—Carissa, thirty-five, from Chicago

"An architect boss once told me to always dress the home in one's most flattering colors. I've painted my homes in Tuscany autumn and coral colors ever since."

—Lana, twenty-nine, from Los Angeles

"We picked out fabric for curtains first, purple with small accents of yellow, then selected paint to match. We chose a yellow that matched those accents *exactly*. Somewhere throughout the process we forgot to look at the big picture— we had painted our walls school-bus yellow! Later, we picked a color we actually liked and painted the walls a beautiful gold, which complements the fabric."

—Kristen, twenty-seven, from Greenville, South Carolina

"Last time my husband bought paint, he chose a really dark orange for the bathroom. We took digital photos of the room and in Photoshop changed the colors of the walls and realized it would be way too overpowering. Technology saved the day!"

—*Justine, thirty-one, from Mountain View, California*

"I bought two to three shades of yellow, then mixed them until I got a shade I liked. Then, took it to a paint store and had them match it."

—*Meryl, twenty-nine, from Oakland, California*

"I got the idea for the colors in our bathroom—dark brown, steel blue, and silver sponge-painted over white—from a Picasso print my husband has."

—*Melina, thirty-three, from Danbury, Connecticut*

light versus dark hues

Once you have a sense of which colors you're drawn to, it's time to determine what interior designers call the color's "value," which essentially boils down to how light or dark you wish the color to be. You can change the value of any hue simply by adding white, which will make the color look more pastel or pearly, or by adding black or gray, which will give the color a darker tint.

Choosing the value of your color becomes extremely important because it plays a huge role in the overall effect of a room once color is on the walls. Those of you who've painted before already know that the color up on the walls always looks darker than the swatch you picked up at the paint store. For that reason Zoe, thirty-three, from Dallas, always errs on the side of "too light" as opposed to "too dark" when choosing colors.

In general, darker values make a room feel more enclosed, which can be cozy, not claustrophobic, while lighter values tend to open up a space, which can be airy, not vast. You can use value as a decorating trick if you wish to make a small room seem larger—by going with a lighter version of it—or a giant room feel more intimate by choosing a darker value. Another trick some designers use is to paint one wall of a room either a darker or lighter hue than the others to bring about a desired effect. For instance, a long narrow room might sport darker hues on one or both of the end walls to bring those walls inward and give the room a less galley-like feel.

In determining the value of your color, it's very important to consider how much natural light the room gets, as well as what time of day you'll be spending most of your time there. That's because natural light will affect the value of the color. In a room that only sees artificial light, a dark tone may feel oppressive to you during the day. Or, it may be the cave you've always dreamed of, depending on your preferences. A room that gets ample sunlight throughout the day may be able to handle darker hues if that's what you're drawn to. Or, the contrast of bright sunlight and dark walls might feel a bit unsettling, according to your tastes. If you plan on spending most of your time in a certain room during the evening, say your bedroom, the natural light factor might play less of a role in your decision, since there won't be any to contend with.

Since ceilings never see natural light, they will appear darker than the walls if you paint them the same color. If you want to exaggerate the height of the ceilings, consider painting them a light neutral, or a halftone of the hue you've chosen for the walls.

🐦 *Roomie Advice: When Tastes Clash* 🐦

Since differences in tastes are a common dynamic among co-habitants, it's best to come up with strategies on how you'll handle the conflict ahead of time. When my husband and I disagree on colors (and when do we not?), we begrudgingly kiss our favorites good-bye and keep going through samples until we finally find a color we can both live with.

Another solution that may work: Each person picks the color for certain rooms. (Just hope those rooms don't begin to resemble a bag of M&M's when you take in the big picture.)

Hannah, thirty-four, from Van Nuys, California, came up with this solution since her husband is drawn to bright hues, and she prefers muted: "I let my husband pick the final color between three or four preapproved by me so he doesn't feel emasculated."

Drew, thirty-three, from New Hartford, New York, admits: "I just dominate. I try to be nice about it."

clear versus muted

In addition to value, a third consideration when choosing a color is the hue's intensity, another interior designer keyword, which basically means how clear or pure the color is in relation to its primary or secondary relative. The closer the color is to its true blue, yellow, orange, red, or green base, the more intense the hue. Rooms in which the colors are all high intensity are usually bright, cheery rooms (think of LEGOs, Crayola's basic set, or Mondrian's grid-like compositions in primary colors).

Toning down the intensity of a color is often wise in rooms that are small or meant for relaxation, since intense colors have a way of energizing rather than calming. Low-intensity colors are usually a subtler version of the original and pleasing when covering large expanses of wall. They yield a soothing effect.

Color swatches usually provide a variety of intensities as well as values (the two are often confused) for a single hue. The difference between value and intensity has to do with the purity of color. To darken a color's value, one simply adds black or gray. Toning down the intensity, however, is achieved by adding a touch of the color's complementary, or opposite, hue on the color wheel. The effect is one of a smokier or muted version of the original, instead of just darker.

The complement of red, for instance, is green. So adding a touch of green to a pure red will dim its intensity and give it a more subtle adobelike shade. The complement of yellow is blue, so if you want to mute the electricity of yellow, add a touch of blue—but not too much or you'll end up with green. Of course, you will most likely not be mixing the paint yourself, but being aware of your preferences in the purity department might help you make a decision when you're faced with thousands of yellows at the paint store.

The climate in which you live might be wise to consider when deciding how pure you want to go in your color choices. "When you go to Mexico and you're surrounded in bright sun, you can wear pure, vibrant colors because they look good down there," says Puhalla. "But in more temperate climates, bright colors often look garish." Same goes with the colors in your home, she says. "If you live in mild climates that have diffuse light, like foggy San Francisco, soft muted colors look good under that light."

So, in hot, sunny climates—the Southwest, Florida, or parts of southern California, intense colors might make perfect sense for your nest. If you live in areas that get softer light due to fog, smog, or high-rise buildings, low-intensity colors might work better—especially if your nest gets to see natural light now and then.

in harmony with your nest

A final consideration when choosing the colors for your nest is the style you're aiming for. Angela, thirty-four, from Houston, wanted the colors in her home to honor the Arts and Crafts–style interior of her craftsman bungalow. So she got inspiration for colors by looking at period-specific magazines and books. For exterior colors, she's looking at books and publications, and is also driving around her neighborhood to see what looks good together.

I also have an Arts and Crafts–style bungalow and wanted to pick colors that were true to the year 1914, when the house was built. Having no idea what those were, my husband and I looked through books, then hit the paint stores and found that many stores have "Historical Palettes" to help customers with this very sort of thing. Sherwin-Williams even had an "Arts and Crafts" palette, and although we only ended up loving one color on the palette (which we used in our bedroom), it was nice to get a sense of what the color scheme was all about—muted, dark colors that are found in nature. In the end, we rationalized that our house wasn't a "true" craftsman, but more of a funky Berkeley bungalow, and that gave us the freedom to go with lighter, brighter tones that wouldn't cut it inside a "true" craftsman.

A final note on choosing colors: Don't forget that paint stores are your friends and they are there to give you guidance as well as sell you paint. "I knew I wanted a cozy, warm red home office and a yellowish beige for the family room, but couldn't figure out how to choose from so many samples," says Sarah, thirty-six, from Kailua, Hawaii. "So I asked the paint store owner which colors people usually ended up with after they had sampled all the others, and I went with the colors she suggested. Now, people always ask me what my colors are so they can use them, too."

Sandra, thirty, from Walnut Creek, California, got more help than she expected from her local paint store: "My boyfriend entrusted me with choosing paint for our new house," she says, "and it has brought out all the worst of my obsessive-compulsive personality. I went into one of the neighborhood paint stores and the woman was over-the-top in her eagerness to help me. She even drove me to her own home to show me how certain colors looked on the wall."

Reese, twenty-nine, from Cleveland, Ohio, was also saved by the paint store. While she had colors in mind, inspired by her dining-room rug, she didn't know if they'd all work together in the same house (she has an open floor plan, so she can see all the colors from one room. At the paint store, she discovered that some of the sample cards suggested color combinations. "It just so happened that the navy we had painted the dining room was on one of the cards, and they had matched purple and gold with it, which were the colors in the rug," she says. "So those were the colors we went with. Our house is now filled with color and I love it. Sometimes I just sit in my chair that has a view of all the different rooms and just drink in how nice it looks."

color theory

Once you've got a sense of colors that you'd like inside of your nest, a quick lesson in color theory might give you a sense of what to do with them. Granted, there are entire books and course work devoted to the subject, so consider this snippet just an introduction to the school of thought rather than a dissertation—if you're interested, check out the resources in the back of the book for more extensive reads.

Color theory is the study of colors and how they combine to make others, as well as how they relate to each other. Painters, textile artists, and interior designers all know the principles, which are based on the color wheel, which you likely had to draw during art class in fourth grade.

The color wheel is based on the three primary colors—yellow, blue, and red—which are equidistant from each other on the wheel. Those three colors combine in various arrangements to create the three secondary colors—green, violet, and orange—which fall between the two parent primary colors on the wheel. Tertiary, or intermediate, colors are the third group of colors on the wheel—yellow-green, blue-green, blue-violet, red-violet, red-orange, and yellow-orange—and they result from the combination of a primary and secondary color that is adjacent on the wheel.

What does this have to do with painting your walls? Well, you can use the color wheel to help determine what colors work in various combinations. This will help you decide what hues work together in one room, what colors are good accents to your wall choice, and what hues might be pleasing from one room to another, say a hallway that leads into two bedrooms.

the harmonious scheme

In such a color scheme, you'll be picking colors that are adjacent to one another on the color wheel—burnt-orange walls, with brick-red and gold accents on the trim and furnishings, for instance. These colors work well together because they're so closely related on the color wheel—they are all warm tones.

Another harmonious scheme might include buttery-yellow walls with sage-green trim (my favorite combination for kitchens). Here, both tones share yellow undertones, which make them work well together. Harmonious color schemes are easy for big-picture planning. In other words, having adjacent rooms in harmonious colors prevents one room from competing with the other, because the two colors blend so well together.

the contrasting scheme

Another pleasing color scheme that perhaps offers a little more drama to a room is one in which the dominant hues are contrasting colors, which means they lie directly opposite of each other on the color wheel. Red and green are a perfect example—we all know how visually exciting red ornaments are on a dark green Christmas tree. But the contrast needn't be so bold as that—adobe walls with accents of blue-green is a subtler version of that combination. Lavender walls work wonderfully with golden accents around the room in curtains, bedspreads, or throw rugs. Since the combination is so lively, it's often best to choose one color as the main hue, then use the contrasting hue for support.

If your heart is set on painting two rooms next to one another in contrasting hues, they may appear to compete with one another, since the combination is so vibrant. To avoid this, be careful to match the colors' intensities. That way, one room won't appear more "pure" or vibrant than the other, and you'll reduce that competitive feel.

the monochromatic scheme

In this scheme, the color wheel isn't necessary, because you just use one predominant color—remember Calvin Klein's White-on-White campaign in the late '90s?

To make this scheme work, though, you will need to vary the values and intensities of the hue you choose, as well as the textures around the room. For instance, combine navy blues with clear light blues with smoky aqua blues, accenting the room with black or white trim and a mix of fabric types—silk, linen, wool. Otherwise, you'll end up with a very flat room that offers no visual or sensual interest.

The monochromatic scheme works well from one room to another, since you're only dealing with one family of color, but to keep each room interesting, the variation in tone is critical—keep some of the rooms a cool blue, for instance, and others a penetrating midnight blue.

the pastel scheme

Finally, there's the Shabby Chic look—decorating a room with pastels of all colors, which gives the mood a romantic, old-fashioned feel. Because the colors are all muted with white (the common denominator), you won't end up with a room that resembles a gumball machine. Instead, you'll be living inside of a Monet.

a note on neutrals

After all this talk of color, I just wanted to make it clear that there is nothing unsensual about a neutral decorating scheme—white, beige, or tan walls offer rooms a blank canvas effect, an unencumbered backdrop to all your furnishings and trinkets.

The simplicity and minimalist quality is often refreshing, especially inside seaside cottages with views of the ocean, in my opinion.

And the light neutral tones often reflect any natural sunlight that enters the room, expanding the space and bringing the outdoors in.

But, if you go with a neutral scheme, consider the advice I've offered under the monochromatic section above. Varied textures and colorful accents are important for giving neutral schemes a sensual, homey feel. Otherwise, you'll end up with a flat, lifeless room.

Blanca, twenty-eight, from Exeter, New Hampshire, went with a neutral scheme in her current apartment—she had wanted color on the walls, but her husband convinced her that muted neutrals would work better because their apartment is small. Crazy colors might make it seem smaller. So, they picked hues that would evoke a mellow, comfortable ambiance and have a nice flow from room to room.

In the living room, they chose a warm, dark ivory with hints of butterscotch. For the ceiling, they opted for an off-white ivory (which was less "white" than they had expected judging from the sample, but turned out to complement the walls tremendously). To add a clean, fresh look to the muted neutrals, they painted the trim a bright, pure white.

In their guestroom, they wanted a subtle sage on the walls, but ended up with a color that turned robin's-egg blue once they got it all up on the wall. To tone it down, they painted the trim the off-white ivory they had used on the ceiling in the living room. For the ceiling, they picked a bright white. That didn't seem to quiet the blue, so they repainted the walls to the sage they had originally wanted, and the result, says Blanca, has an antique-y feel that's welcoming and comfortable.

NESTING PLEASURES:
STENCIL YOUR WALLS

Materials:

Stencil pattern and brush (available at arts and crafts stores)

Masking or painter's tape

Artist's acrylic or latex paint

1. Select the wall area or object you wish to stencil. Common spots include: the area just above a half wall of wainscoting, the border where walls meet ceiling, the transition edge between a two-toned wall, and along the edges of window and door frames. On furniture, the flat faces of drawers and the tops of wooden chests or stools are natural spots for stenciled designs. Even wooden floors are fair game.

2. Prep the area by cleaning the wall with TSP or similar grease and dirt removal. If you're stenciling directly onto unfinished wood, clean with a mild wood soap; when dry, lightly sand using a fine-grit sandpaper—this raises the wood grain so the paint more easily absorbs. (In woods with lots of knots or large grain, you may wish to seal the wood first, then stencil, for a more polished look.)

3. If you are stenciling a border along your wall, measure the space to determine the start and end placements of your stencil. Since you will be reusing the stencil as you go, it's wise to run the pattern along the area you're stenciling, to make sure the ends meet in pleasing ways. If you're placing the

stencils in a geometric pattern along the wall, measure carefully where each design should lie before beginning.

4. Tape the stencil to the wall or furniture piece. Then, dip your stencil brush into the first color of paint you wish to use. Blot excess on a paper towel before brushing the paint into the pattern in a circular motion. If you're using more than one color, add the other colors in the same manner (use a different brush for each color to simplify), being careful not to touch the wet areas you've already done.

5. When the pattern is filled in, carefully lift it off the wall and move it to the next space you wish to stencil. If your pattern repeats and you're making a continuous border, place the stencil so that one of the designs overlaps a design you just painted. With those matching, you'll be sure to continue the border without any weird blips in rhythm.

6. In general, you won't need to apply a topcoat of varnish over stenciling on wall surfaces, but if you're stenciling wood or furniture, such as a frame, a chest, an old bureau, it's a good idea to paint a layer of varnish or sealant after the paint has dried for extra protection.

on purchasing paint

Before you run out to the paint store and buy five gallons of what looks like the "perfect" tone, there is one more mandatory step—testing the color on your walls. Testing your paint pick is highly recommended.

I write this not only based on my personal experience but also on what I heard during the many interviews I did on the subject. It will save you time and money, and in the end, you'll end up with the best color for your rooms. If my husband and I hadn't tested the burnt-orange "Persimmons" sample we thought we adored for our bedroom, we would be falling asleep in what we quickly came to call "Pepto-Bismol," which is what the color looked like once we painted a quarter of one wall with the sample we bought.

Always, always, always buy a pint-sized sample of your top pick to test in the room *before* you begin to paint the entire thing. I know that means two trips to the paint store instead of one, which is a drag, but there are two very good reasons for this:

1. Paint on the wall always looks different from the paint on the swatch. Typically, it's darker and more intense once you get a lot of paint up—something you can never judge with a two-inch sample taped to the middle of a white wall.
2. Paint colors change throughout the day, depending upon how much natural light falls on it. In most cases, the undertones shine through more clearly once sunlight hits the color, which changes the overall effect. In our case, the pinkish undertones that had escaped our notice on the sample became the dominant hue once we got the color up on the wall of our sunny room.

Since sunlight will hit your walls in different amounts and at different times of day, it's a good idea to test this color on several walls in the room you wish to paint. Jackie, thirty-two, from El Dorado, California, offers this advice from experience: "Paint your sample on a large piece of butcher paper instead of the wall itself." That way, you can move the paper around to different walls during different times of the day.

She discovered this tactic after she painted a test splotch on one of her walls. Her painting plans were unexpectedly interrupted for several months, and she had to live with the splotch on the wall for longer than she would have liked. Also, if you get a sample up there that you instantly hate, you can easily remove the paper until you find the color you do like.

Once you've determined the color, you will need to determine the type of paint—oil or latex, flat or glossy. Unless you are planning on experimenting with a faux finish that works best with an oil-based paint base (more on this in a minute), latex paints are the way to go. Latex, or water-based paints, are less toxic, quicker to dry, cheaper, and much easier to clean. And the quality is indistinguishable from that of an oil-based paint. It is what most people use when painting their interiors. Of the latex paints, you have several choices of finish, the most common being matte or flat, semigloss, and gloss.

Matte or flat finishes are what you most commonly see on home walls—they give balanced and peaceful textures and help hide small blemishes. Semigloss or high gloss, depending on how much shine you're after, are common picks for woodwork around the house—baseboards, built-in cabinets and shelves, and window trim—because the glossier latex paints are more durable against nicks and easier to clean (whatever chemicals produce the sheen also hold up better to cleaning products than a flat finish, which may eventually wear away). Because of its easy-cleaning properties, semigloss is often the preferred finish for kitchen and bathroom walls, which see more splatters and residue than, say, the living-room walls. Glossier finishes also reflect more light, so in some cases that may be more desirable if, for instance, you're going for an ultramodern sensibility in your sleek and shiny nest.

When ordering paint, always ask for high-quality paint, which is only a little more expensive than its cheaper cousin. Ask the paint store clerk what they recommend. High quality will mean that you have to paint less, because the paint absorbs better into the wall. So, even though you may be paying more per gallon, you'll likely end up paying less overall, because you may only need to do one coat instead of three.

prepping and painting

Prepping a wall before you paint is the final step before adding color to your nest. It's not one to skip, even though it's a complete bore and often takes more time to do than the actual painting. But, a prepped wall will make painting easier and will look better in the end.

The first step is to remove all nails and art-hanging fixtures, as well as electrical outlets and light switch covers (put masking tape over the remaining plastic switches and outlets so you won't splash paint on those—a minor detail that can avoid an ugly and obvious blemish). If you have sconces on the wall, you'll want to turn off your electricity and remove these, too, taping the ends of live wires just in case you need to turn the electricity back on while the paint dries.

Next, you'll want to clean the walls of dirt and grease with TSP or a similar product and a sponge or rag (ask your paint store for suggestions). When dry, use ready-made spackling to cover any cracks and or nail holes (buy a spackling spatula for application). After about an hour, when the spackling has set, lightly sand off any excess with a sheet of medium- or fine-grit sandpaper. Wipe off the white dust that results with a damp cloth. Finally, you'll want to place painter's tape or masking tape along the trim and edges of the wall, where you don't want the new paint to bleed or drip onto. Then, spread newspaper or a drop cloth on the floor and you're ready to begin.

With the actual painting, it's always a good idea to prime the walls first with a high-quality primer (again, ask paint store clerks for their suggestions). Primer is a thick white paint-like substance that's good to use when you have a newly plastered wall or are trying to paint a light color over a dark one.

The primer helps the real paint color adhere better to the wall, giving it a more even finish, and it helps prevent an old color from bleeding through to the new one. Meryl, twenty-nine, from Oakland, California, suggests having the primer tinted with the same color you are planning on using on the walls. "It makes a great base," she says. "You'll only have to do one final coat of paint."

Once the primer has dried, you're ready for the color. If it's been a while since you've painted (or you've never done it before), you'll want a two-to-three-inch brush for cutting in, a little pail, a roller with extension if you have high walls or plan to paint the ceiling, a ladder, and a paint tray. In general, you'll use the roller to get most of the paint on the wall or ceiling, then use your brush and pail (so you don't have to haul around a whole gallon of paint) to cut in, or fill in the edges and corners where the roller couldn't reach.

As you get that color up, don't freak out if you begin to have second thoughts. "When you first put color on a wall, it always looks really drastic and crazy—especially if you're coming from white walls," says Meryl. "Wait until the paint is on all walls and has dried, and you've moved your furniture in. Then, you'll see the whole room, and the color won't appear so dominating."

HOW TO THROW A PAINT PARTY

First, the reality: When you invite your friends over to paint your walls, you may not get them painted in the exact way you might have done so solo. The perks, of course, are that you get the room painted much quicker and with a lot more spirit than you would doing the work all by your lonesome. If you go the communal route, you must place the emphasis on party—how else are you going to beg your friends for their help? Party tips are as follow:

1. Beverages and food: The essential components of a successful paint party. Pizza and good beer (not Bud in a can) are common favorites, but you can also go a little more gourmet, if you please, with homemade lasagna (an easy, filling fix for large crowds) or some variation of your favorite pasta salad. For added inspiration, consider a cocktail that matches the color you're painting—Cosmos for a pink bedroom; Mojitos for a kelly-green kitchen. Warning: You might want to introduce the heavy liquor when you're wrapping up. Otherwise, the paint job will suffer.

2. Snacks: In addition to a lunch or dinner meal, keep a healthy supply of snacks around your nest for that spurt of energy your guests and laborers will need to get the job done. Chocolate is always a good call. Chips will do the trick, too.

3. Good music: Essential for keeping the party lively. Don't forget to take pictures—grooving to the tunes while painting is sure to occur among several of your guests.

4. Painting supplies for all: You will need at least one roller or brush for every participant, which is why it is wise to keep the guest list small—unless you plan to paint a whole nest in one day, in which case, you'll also need supplies for every room. Your guests can trade off tasks when they get sick of cutting in or rolling on paint.

5. A plan: Just as you might plan the general flow of a dinner party (guests arrive, cocktails for all, dinner is served, dessert by the fire), so must you prepare a general plan for painting or else mayhem could occur. If you're attempting the works—ceilings, walls, and trim—get your guests started on cutting in and rolling on the paint of both the ceilings and the walls—scatter them about so no one runs into each other. Two people per wall or ceiling is a good number for starters— they can begin on opposite sides and meet in the middle.

Since you may need to tape between wall and ceiling, depending on whether or not you have molding between the two, you may need to start and finish one or the other first, then move onto the next when the paint has dried. Save the trim for last, since glossier finishes tend to dry more slowly. If your party is a daylong event, schedule the walls and ceiling in the morning (after coffee and pastries, of course), then break for lunch while those dry. Then, tackle the trim in the afternoon.

6. A place for guests to clean: Always offer your shower to guests who offer their help at a paint party. Be prepared with a slew of clean towels, soaps, and postshower primping—pull out your best lotions and hair products. Then, get out of the

house—the fumes are likely getting to all of you and fresh evening air is in order. Planning something afterward—a movie, dinner, or even a swim (if it's the right season) is a great way to end the backbreaking day.

decorative tricks

Last but not least, a word on faux paint finishes. You've likely seen them on restaurant walls or inside the nests of your very crafty friends. A decorative paint finish gives texture and depth to a wall, unlike a flat paint job. It relies on the interaction of two colors—the base coat, which is painted like a normal wall, and the top finish, which is a glaze that allows the under color to seep through.

The glaze is applied using various techniques. The play of color not only adds visual excitement but also movement within a room, doubling the sensuality appeal. What follows are details of the easier faux finishes to achieve.

Sponging

Because this finish works well in latex paints, it's one I would recommend for beginners—simply because the cleanup is so much easier than it would be working in oil-based paints, and if your walls are already painted in latex (likely), you might be able to avoid repainting that first coat if you're happy with the current color as a base.

As with all faux paint jobs, you'll start with a base coat in the color you wish to be less dominant—this will be the color that peeks through the top glaze, giving your room an under-glow. Some nice examples that I've seen are base coats in burnt orange, with the glaze in yellow. Or, base coats in blue and the glaze in sea green, which yields a patina look.

Once the base coat is dry, you'll be using a sea sponge (available at most paint stores) to apply a latex glaze, tinted in the second color you've picked for this finish. (Note: You can make your own latex glaze by adding two parts latex paint in the top color you desire, to one part water. Mix these together in a bucket, then pour into a painter's pan for easy access.)

Then, don some latex gloves so you don't get paint all over your hands, and dip the sponge into the glaze. Blot the sponge on a thick stack of paper towels, until the paint appears evenly on the part of the sponge that will touch the wall, then pat the glaze onto the wall in a rhythmic pattern around the room, being careful not to smudge the pattern as you move across the wall. Re-dip the sponge in the glaze when needed, but always blot before you tackle the wall or you'll get an uneven look. You can apply the glaze as densely to the base coat as you like—the idea is to have just a hint of the original color shine through. Tear off a smaller part of the sponge to reach the corners and edges, where two walls meet—both of which are easy targets for smearing. For a polished look, place masking tape along adjacent walls while you're working, so you won't have any unplanned blotches to contend with.

I've also seen beautiful sponging techniques in which the sponge is immersed in paint, blotted, and then rolled across the wall, giving the pattern a more organic look. The key to sponging (and all decorative finishes) is to approach the task with confidence. Remember, if you screw up an area, you can always repaint that bit with the undercoat, then reapply the glaze when that has dried. Once it has dried, you'll never notice the difference.

Ragging, Dragging, or Stippling

In these finishes, which are often best with oil-based paints, you'll first paint a base coat in one color, then when dry, you'll paint an oil-based glaze in another color on top.

For ragging, you'll need a healthy supply of clean rags that don't have lint. Scrunch up a rag while the glaze is still wet, and lightly roll it across the wall, picking up glaze along the way, so the under color shines through in an even texture. When the rag becomes saturated with glaze, turn it over and inside out. Eventually, you'll need to swap for a new rag. (It's best to work in two- or three-foot sections in this technique. Just re-rag over any overlapping parts when you apply new glaze.)

For dragging, you'll apply the glaze first, then use a dry paintbrush to sweep through it, leaving brush streaks along the way, and letting the base coat seep through. Hint: Keep the brush on the wall for the length of the wall to avoid any obvious breaks. Also, keep some clean rags around so you can wipe off the brush when it becomes too full of glaze—the key to mastering this texture is keeping the brush dry.

Stippling is very similar to dragging, in that you're using a dry paintbrush to create texture in the glaze, but in this finish, you'll apply the glaze to the wall, and then bounce the brush atop it while it's still wet in various patterns around the room, instead of sweeping it through. The effect offers a more randomized texture than dragging, which looks very linear.

Color Washing

This is another easy finish to achieve using a water-based or latex glaze, and it's one that's often used on unfinished wood. The effect is one of distressed wood, so it has a bit of an antique-y feel. If you're starting with unfinished wood—wainscoting, trim, or even a chest of drawers—all you need to do is clean the surface with mineral spirits, then when it's dry, flood the area with the glaze using a brush. Next, quickly wipe off the glaze with a clean, lint-free cloth, rubbing hard over any knots or moldings where the glaze might have absorbed more deeply. You'll end up with a tinted shade of wood, grain and knots still exposed.

Laura, thirty-two, from Warren, Michigan, used a version of color washing in her kitchen. She calls it the "Oh My God, That Color Is Totally Orange, We Have to Wipe It Off Before It Dries!" technique. The original walls, she says, were light chiffon yellow, until she and her husband decided to punch up the color with "Marigold." After one coat of regular latex paint, they realized their error and quickly wiped off the paint with wet rags. The original yellow peeked through, and they loved the effect.

Another way to color wash is to use a brush. Simply apply the glaze very thinly with a brush in a hatch-marked pattern, changing the direction of your stroke so you're left with lots of obvious, angular brush marks. Be sure to apply the glaze lightly, so the under color shines through.

A BIT ON WALLPAPER

In researching, I watched a *Better Homes and Garden* video on wallpapering, and the whole thing made me so nervous I had to turn the VCR off!

The measuring of wall space, the calculating of panels, the wall prep, the idea of keeping each panel straight—I couldn't get to the end of this video, because even the demonstrator was having problems around the corner moldings of windows and door frames. If he was fumbling, how in the heck could amateurs like us paper an entire room on a lazy Saturday afternoon?

While wallpaper does have an antiquated quality to it, I recommend a faux paint job instead. Not only is it easier to achieve, but paint finishes give depth to a room where wallpaper can't, because wallpaper is a flat print.

6

Textiles

*Composed of grasses, bark, moss, and cloth bound with mud,
the cup-like nest of the Wood Thrush is shaped by the contours
of the female's body.*

 Textiles offer the nest several layers of sensuality—visual stimulation in the form of color, sheen, and patterns, tactile stimulation from the feel of different fibers and various weaves, even olfactory appeal from the subtle scent of wool or silk and the dyes used on them. If you've ever buried your nose into a hand-dyed batik sarong, you'll know what I'm talking about.

Upholstered furniture, wall tapestries, throw pillows and blankets, tablecloths, rugs, and curtains—a nest is not a nest without textiles, which do so much to personalize and privatize a space.

White billowy drapes, for instance, quietly frame a tranquil garden view, while a bold Roman blind, kept closed, offers a stimulating alternative to the toxic wasteland across the street. Pastel-striped silk throw pillows offer a touch of sheen and softness to a couch covered in leather or wool. A jute throw rug provides a rustic introduction in the entryway of your casual-country nest. A floor-length pale green linen tablecloth may offer the precise touch of formality to an otherwise plain-Jane dining nook.

Like paint colors on the wall, choosing fabrics for your nest can be a daunting experience—especially when it comes to coordinating patterns with solids, not to mention choosing from the many natural and synthetic fibers out there.

But with a systematic approach, weaving these textiles into your nest not only yields a sensual space that's neither too busy nor too dull but it can also be fun.

how to weave a room

One of the snags to choosing textiles for the nest is the insecurity and overwhelming fatigue so many of us feel when we step into a fabric store. The sensation is not unlike the panic we experience at Sherwin-Williams regarding paint color choices.

Is this paisley silk pattern too busy for an occasional chair? How will this pale yellow wool look on a throw pillow atop my sage-green sofa? It's enough to send us scurrying back to the Pottery Barn catalogue to stick with basic beige twill for every textile in the house.

I truly admire those who aren't afraid of mixing textile patterns and colors and fabric types around their nest. A friend of mine does this beautifully with a gorgeous collection of Turkish rugs and floor pillows, a chair upholstered in a traditional Navajo print, and a variety of mismatched throw pillows and blankets—all in the same space. The rich reds blend beautifully and the patterns seem to have been made for one another, even though they weren't.

Alas, most of us aren't born with the natural talent of "just knowing" what combination of textiles look good in one room. There is a fine line between mixing fabrics artfully and throwing together a tapestry of clashing chaos that makes a room spin. Or on the flip side, creating a nest that's too matchy-matchy . . . and dull.

For starters, narrow down your options by deciding on the type of fabric to use for the particular nesting need in question. There are two categories of fabrics: natural fibers and synthetics.

"When it comes to textiles, I only use natural fibers in the home, not synthetics," says Jennifer Puhalla, an interior designer in San Francisco. "I find that natural fibers have depth, whereas synthetics typically only have sheen. When you stick with natural fibers, you'll automatically have something more successful," she says.

The most common natural fibers found in human nests include cotton, linen, wool, rayon, silk, or a blend of any of the above. Each fiber has its own sensual appeal.

Silk, for instance, gives a furniture piece or a window covering a more formal look, since it has natural luster and is soft and elegant and, for drapes, it hangs well, allowing light to play with its folds.

Silk is one of the more expensive and delicate natural fibers on the market, so it's wise to use sparingly around the nest on pieces that don't receive extensive wear and tear or direct natural light. I've used raw silk as curtains for several of my previous nests. Because these windows never saw direct sunlight, they held up quite well. The sheen even acted as faux sunlight, which brightened up the room.

Taffeta, silk's stronger and sturdier stepsister, often makes a more durable choice for items that beg for the sheen and texture of silk, but need a little more strength. Seat coverings, for instance, hold up better in taffeta than a thin, delicate silk.

Linen, because it wrinkles easily, may appear more casual than silk. But, linen also has a natural luster that can turn a boring set of drapes into a glowing formal window covering. When sunlight shines through linen curtains, the windows practically glow, bringing soft filtered light inside the nest.

On napkins or tablecloths or hand towels or sheets, linen is cool to the touch and keeps its crisp shape well. On bedding, linen sheets stay stiff and cool even during sweltering August nights in Texas.

Cotton, rayon, and wool are the more durable natural fibers and come in a variety of weights and weaves, giving these fabrics a wide range of sensual appeal, from stiff and heavy to feather soft and light.

Typically, each of these fabrics offers a variety of weaves, patterns, colors, and sheens to choose from. Because of their durability, they are often the most versatile and practical natural fibers to use in the nest, though some wool weaves can be scratchy to touch. Upholstered furniture often uses these fabrics. Curtains, throw blankets, and bedding are other popular choices.

Other fibers, such as hemp, jute, and sisal give a rough appearance and texture to a textile and are often great choices for rugs or place mats in the rustic nest.

While natural fibers may weave a more natural nest, I do feel the need to mention synthetics. In fact, some synthetics may be even more suitable to your specific nesting needs than natural fibers. If your nest is home to a pet or toddler, or if you have a sporty lifestyle that involves shuffling bikes, eclectic sporty footwear, and other equipment around the nest, a nylon carpet or rug, for instance, might be a practical choice, since it's easier to clean and more stain resistant than sisal or some wools or cottons. To the untrained eye, they are just as lovely in many cases. Remember from Chapter 4: A clean nest is a sensual nest. If yours is prone to dirt and dust, then synthetics might be the most sensual textile option for you.

Also, points out New York City interior designer Lauri Ward, author of the Use What You Have decorating series, a new and improved generation of synthetic materials has produced very strong and soft synthetic fabrics. Hard performance Ultrasuede and Sunbrella are two examples. "Aesthetics are important when choosing fabrics, but so is functionality," she says. "When I work with clients, I always advise them to go for the fabrics that are flexible and durable for their lifestyles."

Once you've narrowed down your choices in fibers, you are left to pick the colors and possibly patterns for the textiles needed. This is an entirely subjective process, but the following considerations may help guide you to the right choice.

In her line of work, New York City interior designer Judy Sheridan, author of *Instant Décor* and *Winning Windows*, first gets a sense of what her clients are drawn to—plain colors or patterns, earth tones or pastels, bold prints or barely-there geometric designs. From there, she considers the general palette of the room and what aspects of the space define the overall look and feel. Do picture windows call for formal drapery that will dominate the textile offerings in the room? Does an antique Amish quilt hung on the wall serve as the baseline for other fabric picks?

Finally, she considers what "period," if any, her client is aiming to replicate. A Louis XVI look would have her concentrate on the formal fabrics—damasks, silks, and taffetas. The English country style would call for more informal and comfortable textiles such as cotton in a chintz print, checks, or plaids, with pattern piled upon pattern. The Contemporary look may beg for a mix of wool weaves interspersed with smooth textures and for added crunch, unexpected accents, such as mohair or cut velvet.

Then, the task is one of weaving these fabrics in a complementary way, which takes practice and more often than not, trial and error. To begin, choose a dominant textile, then base your other fabric choices around it. If that textile is a striped rug, for instance, use one color within the rug for your curtains. Or, have your throw pillows on the sofa in that tone. If you're planning on reupholstering the couch or making slipcovers, use a different color from the textile to tie these pieces together. Keeping a common tone running throughout the various fabric choices in a space unifies the textiles. So, even if your curtains don't "match" your sofa upholstery, they complement, even enhance each other quite well.

As you weave, keep in mind that it's always a good idea to have a variety of textiles in the nest, says Sheridan. A soft chenille blanket on a cool leather sofa, for instance, adds a touch of warmth and silkiness to an otherwise stiff (but chic) seating nook. A sheepskin rug beneath an armchair upholstered in chintz pattern gives that space an interesting contrast in textures—firm and cool on the body, cozy and toe gripping on the feet.

By the way, always test a textile in your home before purchasing yards and yards, advises Melina, thirty-three, from Danbury, Connecticut. "I have fabric stores clip anything I'm interested in. Some of the colors look really yellowish under the store lights, but are gorgeous in my home, so you have to keep testing," she says.

If the clipping is too small to tell how it might look spread over, say, your sofa, go ahead and buy one yard—or at least half a yard if you have strong doubts. "You want to make sure you can handle large amounts of the colors," says Sarah, thirty-six, from Kailua, Hawaii.

cotton versus silk: what goes where?

Every room in the nest needs textiles—bedding in the boudoir, shower curtains in the bath, linens in the dining area, dish towels in

THE PERFECT MATCH

Picking fabrics isn't a science, as these women reveal.

"I chose the upholstery on my couch by taking samples, rubbing them on my cat, and picking the one that showed her hair the least."

—*Claire, thirty-five, from Bellingham, Washington*

"I loved an old shirt that my husband was going to chuck, so I cut it up and put it on a chair. It looks good and adds color."

—*Laura, thirty-two, from Warren, Michigan*

"My chartreuse kitchen table chairs need recovering, but their vinyl is very distinctive. I researched online and found a matching pattern, but in a different color."

—*Lola, thirty-two, from Olympia, Washington*

"I go to the Metropolitan Museum and look at the collection of old seventeenth- and eighteenth-century dresses for inspiration—especially for window coverings. I've developed details for trim and ideas for valences based on old French dresses."

—*Judy Sheridan, founder of*
Sheridan Interiors, Inc., of Manhattan

> "I make one fabric dominant in a given space. It's great when it's bold and dramatic. Then for a tailored look, I use a complementary solid for each patterned fabric."
>
> —Meryl, twenty-nine, from Oakland, California

the kitchen, curtains and throw pillows and rugs in the living area. Each specific nesting item has a wide range of choice in colors, patterns, and textures. To simplify the process of choosing textiles for these specific items, here is the lowdown on a few staples in the home.

Sofa and Chair Upholstery

Luckily, there is a wide range of textiles sturdy enough to withstand the necessary wear and tear of seating furniture. Among the natural fibers, soft and durable wool, linen, and cotton are top contenders. If the wear and tear is extreme—from pets or toddlers or your own rough-and-tumble lifestyle—microfibers, such as Ultrasuede, may be your best option for keeping the piece(s) from becoming too shabby too soon.

Of course, leather is another option. Though not technically a textile but a hide, leather is one of the most stain-resistant, sturdy seat coverings out there. The only problem with leather is that it's not usually very cozy. If you're the type to curl up in your couch for afternoon naps, a cotton, linen, or wool-covered couch might be the better choice for you.

As for color, it's generally wise to stick with dark tones. These show stains less and tend to have a longer life. And the unanimous response from the decorators I interviewed was to steer clear of bold designs on the sofa. It's hard to use a bold, big, overblown pattern on such a big piece of furniture. And then there's the risk of falling for a short-lived trend: "You'll tire of a busy pattern," warns interior designer Lauri Ward, "but solids never go out of style."

Lana, twenty-nine, from Los Angeles, learned the hard way: "Colorful flowers may look nice on a showroom sofa, but when someone wearing plaid sits down on my couch, my stomach turns over." She suggests saving colored patterns for curtains and bedspreads. Or, use them on throw pillows and blankets, which are great tools for adding visual and tactile interest to a solid-colored chair or sofa.

If your eye begs for pattern, stripes usually work well without dominating the room. And so does damask—tone-on-tone coloration works beautifully. Textures with checks or diamonds that come from the weave of the textile's fibers rather than color is another way to add visual interest to an otherwise plain-colored covering.

TO SLIPCOVER OR NOT

Slipcovers come in two flavors: the Cover-the-Entire-Sofa-or-Chair Type and the Slip-Over-the-Cushions-Only Type. Nesters all seem to have different opinions about using them. Some, like Amanda, twenty-seven, from Chicago, contend that they always slide and look uneven. "Loose-fit slipcovers only look good when you first put them on and tuck them in. I had a couple covering some god-awful pink couches, and as soon as anyone sat down, they came untucked. Although the color was less offensive, the couch still looked very messy." Oh, and unless you're crafty, she warns, don't fool yourself into thinking you can make your own.

Others, however, have had more luck with slipcovers. Maria, thirty, from Brooklyn, has used them on some of the secondhand furniture she inherited from family. "I ordered them off the Internet. They are so much cheaper and such better quality than those from department stores. I wouldn't pay less than $200 per cover, and I wouldn't go over $350."

If you go with a slipcover option, find out the cleaning instructions. You want to be sure that the covers won't shrink in the wash, since the point of using them is to be able to clean them easily.

Throw Pillows and Blankets

Pillows and blankets are the ideal recipient of bold designs or poppy colors. "Patterns are wonderful on throw pillows," says interior designer Judy Sheridan. "Especially if the pattern has an unexpected quality, for example, a chintz pattern that's not centered on the pillow but kept off to the side."

She also loves stripes on throw pillows or those that are made from more than one fabric. Silk adds a touch of sheen and softness to a utilitarian couch or armchair. Detailed needlepoint pillows add a homemade element of craftsmanship.

Molly, thirty-two, from San Francisco, has many throw pillows in her nest. Handmade from various fabrics and beads, she keeps a stack of them on the floor next to an armchair for extra seating.

Besides adding color to a room or area, throw pillows are great for pulling together a color scheme. Making covers for your throw pillows out of the same fabric as your curtains can really tie a room together. Or, making throw pillows out of one accent color from a dominant throw rug in front of the sofa can also pull the rug and sofa together in a subtle but electric way.

When purchasing throw pillows, don't forget to weigh in the comfort factor. If you like to scrunch up your pillows and wedge them behind your neck as you sprawl across the sofa watching *Saturday Night Live,* go for the more sturdy cotton blends. They are soft and cozy, but can withstand twisting and squishing much better than, say, silk or lace or delicate embroidery.

As for blankets, a chenille throw is soft and cozy for winter nights. Katie, twenty-six, from Chicago, says the warm throw on her couch is the one thing she looks forward to after a busy day at work. Blankets with Celtic or Navajo designs add a spark of geometric interest to a plain-clothed sofa. And for contrast, homemade quilts bring a little bit of country into rock-and-roll urban nests.

One of the great things about throw pillows and blankets is that they can be updated and interchanged whenever your seating area needs a fresh look. Instead of periodically swapping slipcovers or reupholstering, you can simply (and cheaply) change to a new color or design.

Window Coverings

The textile options for window coverings are so plentiful that rows of books dedicated to the subject line the shelves of bookstores and libraries. For the purposes of this book, I'll narrow down your options to a sensual few: shades, blinds, and curtains.

Shades are one of the cheapest textiles available for covering your

NESTING PLEASURES: THE HOME-AWAY-FROM-HOME SWATCH

So you'll never have to guess how that chartreuse linen throw pillow will look in your sort-of-blue bedroom, construct a purse-sized swatch book of all the colors and fabrics in your home.

Materials:
Index cards (five-by-seven-inch)
Paint of all the colors of your walls
Swatches of the fabrics in your home
(Or, pictures of the two items above)
Glue
Punch hole
Binder rings or Velcro tabs
Measuring tape
Pencil

1. Gather the number of index cards that equal the number of rooms or "spaces" in your nest.

2. Paint one side of the card with the dominant color of the walls. If you have a two-tone room, include the two colors proportionately as they appear in the space. If you don't have extra paint, take a photo of the wall, and glue that onto the card. For those with wallpaper, cut out a five-by-seven-inch piece of your remnants and glue it onto the card.

3. If you have remnants of the various fabrics around your rooms, from curtains to slipcovers, cut out a small swatch of

each and glue those onto the card once the paint has dried. Again, if you don't have extra fabric, take a photo and glue a cutout of the pattern on the card. Size these swatches according to their dominance in the room. If you have a wall of curtains, place a larger sample of that fabric on your index card than, say, a tiny silk upholstered occasional chair.

4. Continue on with any other dominant color features in the room that may influence future purchases—a large painting, a wall tapestry, a throw rug, a tablecloth.

5. Do this for each room in your home, then punch a small hole in the corner of each card and bind them together with a binder ring or Velcro tab or even a piece of twine.

6. If you're looking for specific furniture items for a room, jot down the measurements of wall spaces and windows on the back of each card. That way, when you're in an antique shop, you'll know whether a certain china cabinet you're in love with will fit between the two windows in your dining room.

windows and come in a variety of options. Honeycomb shades, made of lightweight polyester, allow natural light to filter through while serving as great insulators.

Roman shades (made of many different materials, from bamboo strips to 100 percent natural cotton) give a clean finish to most windows, with fabric folding in a minimalist way when they are drawn open.

And see-through solar shades, composed of synthetic fibers that block out the glare of sunlight, are ideal choices for rooms with a view.

The bountiful options in the category of shades allow you to choose the exact amount of sunlight you'd like to filter through, including none at all if you opt for black-out fabrics or liners. The simplicity of a shade means that you can downplay the window covering as much as you want, drawing attention to the other sensual aspects of the room. On the other hand, if you want to enhance the window area, a shade is a great medium for showing off bold patterns because it hangs flat when closed, so designs aren't interrupted by folds as they are in curtains.

While shades are effective light-blocking options for your windows, the disadvantage is that you don't have much control over letting light in—the shades are either up or down or somewhere in between (which isn't the greatest look from outside the window, by the way).

A better choice for those who wish to manipulate the amount of light entering a room—the more sensual choice, in my opinion—is to opt for wooden blinds or shutters. While these are not textiles, of course, blinds or shutters offer a clean, minimalist look to a window. Unlike shades, you can change the amount of outside light entering the room by adjusting the slant of the blades—a tilt up or down brings a soft glow of sunlight into the room, enabling you to see outside while maintaining privacy. If wooden blinds are out of budget (and they are expensive), consider curtains or shades instead of the standard issue apartment dwellers' metal blinds. That simple touch can do a lot in terms of personalizing your nest.

Curtains, of course, are the traditional window coverings of homes, but they are also more involved in a decorative sense. Not only must you pick the fabric but also the rod and rings for attaching the material to the wall or window molding.

Valences and all sorts of other decorative features, such as tassels, hooks, lining, and trim, also fall within the equation. The decisions continue: You have several choices for length—sill length, floor length, or somewhere in between—and a variety of methods for opening or tying them back—hooks or tassels?

And, of course, then there's the style of curtain to consider—pleated for a more tailored look or loose and billowy, forming natural peaks and valleys that play with the light.

Let's start with the fabric choices. The first question to ask is how the window is used. If there is a view and the curtain will mainly be drawn open, only closed at night for privacy, you'll want a lightweight fabric that won't billow out, for this could potentially block the view. If the window's main contribution to the nest is leaking warm air out in the winter, a floor-length curtain drawn at night will serve as an excellent insulator.

Velvet, along with cotton (light or heavyweight), wool, linen, silk (as long as it's lined, since direct sunlight can quickly do damage to silk), and rayon all drape well and make stunning fabric choices. Best bet is to take a few samples and hold them up to the window, assessing their drape, capability for blocking or filtering sunlight, and their look when tied back.

Next comes the question of patterns or solids. Here, interior designers have differing opinions. Some contend that a solid color is best, since it won't overpower the room. Solids will put more emphasis on what's outside the window than the window itself, which is great if you have something pleasant to look out onto.

Others, however, contend that curtains are as good a textile as any for defining the color palette and giving the eye a refreshing pop of color or design. Stripes are a common favorite, tying in colors from other textiles in the room. And small prints also often work well, since they won't dominate or compete with other textiles you wish to emphasize.

As for curtain length, really anything goes. Floor-length curtains tend to have a more formal look than those that just brush the edge of the windowsill. Lana, twenty-nine, from Los Angeles, loves the floor-to-ceiling look, but didn't want to spend the big bucks that all that fabric costs. So she hit on the idea to use ten-foot-long brocade tablecloths instead of premade curtains, and her living room windows now have the elegance she desired for a fraction of the cost.

Sill-length curtains, which just brush the edge of the windowsill lip, have a more informal, lighter look, and these are often perfect for kitchens and bathrooms—rooms that receive a lot of wear and tear and aren't exactly the types of spaces where you want a ton of loose fabric that only gathers dust or dirt or grease. Curtains that hang somewhere in between always look a little lost to me, but to each her own.

Finally, consider the rods and rings and how you plan to secure the curtains when open. Ask yourself how often you'll be manipulating them. If your curtains are primarily open, as they often are in the kitchen or entertaining space, it will not matter so much if the rings slide easily across the rod or snag where the rod breaks for adjustment.

If you open and close the curtains frequently, though, as you might in the bathroom or bedroom, be extra careful in choosing your rod and rings—brass, iron, or wooden rods cut to the exact length with matching rings tend to slide smoothly across the rod.

Hooks attached to the window frame to hold the curtain back are also another simple way to draw a curtain—you can open these without dragging the curtains across the rod. Tassels or tiebacks are another option to consider. Katie, twenty-six, from Chicago, uses them: "I had a hard time finding drapes that would fit the width and length of our huge windows, so I bought three panels of drapes and secured each with a tied tassel. At night, we just take the tassels off," she says. She was amazed at what a dramatic statement such a simple window covering could make.

Bedding

When it comes to bedding, the tactile contributions far outweigh the visual appeal, at least in my bedroom. But comfort is extremely subjective. While some equate flannel bedding to nothing less than godly, others find it suffocating to sleep on, preferring the slip-and-slide effect of satin or silk sheets instead.

The most critical aspect of cozy bedding, in my opinion, is the sheets, because these are what envelop you during the night. Your first order of business is to decide what type of material you'd like for your sheets—cotton (which is soft and cool to touch in summer months, but warms up quickly in winter), linen (the sheet of all sheets, according to many bedding enthusiasts, due to its substantial weight, crispness, and durability), silk (which is very expensive and impossible to launder on your own—ideally preserved for very special occasions), and various weaves and blends of cottons and synthetics to create all sorts of textures and weights such as sateen, flannel, and knit.

Firsthand experience with all your choices is the best way to decide what flavor of sheet is right for you. Some find the most sensual beds to be those covered in thick sheets that are crisp and cool to touch. Others prefer satiny sheets that drape luxuriously over the body, allowing totally unrestricted freedom of movement—you never get tangled up in those sheets, but you might slip off the bed if you're not too careful. And many prefer the warmth of flannel in the winter.

If you're unsure of what you like, a safe bet is a basic cotton sheet with a thread count of 180 or more, because these sheets are affordable, long lived, easy to clean and keep fresh, and feel soft on the skin. Typically, the higher the thread count, the less likely you'll wear holes into them with weekly washings and the friction caused by sleeping and . . . whatever else you do in your bed.

Thread counts up to 250 or even higher indicate higher quality sheets (but not always, caveat emptor). Kira, twenty-six, from Seattle, splurges on sheets and always buys at least 300-plus thread count. When she has time, she even irons them to look and feel even shinier and softer.

Shopping for blankets warrants the same criteria—you'll want to assess their softness and weight. Cotton blankets are usually soft to the touch and come in a variety of weights. The lighter weaves and materials, like fleece, are better for those of you who hate feeling pinned down by your covers. Heavier woolen blankets will give you that mummified feeling, if that's your preference.

There are two other points worth discussing in this chapter: the colors of your bedding and the top layer that covers it all up. Let's start with the cover or duvet or quilt—however you choose to wrap up your own unique package of cotton or satin or linen sheets and cotton or wool or fleece blankets.

For starters, it's a good idea to pick the top cover according to the climate in which you live. Florida dwellers rarely need down comforters, unless you are like Reese, twenty-nine, from Cleveland, Ohio, who now resides in Tampa. She and her mate keep the temperature in their bedroom really low, making it the darkest, coolest room in the house, "like a little cave," she says. They top their bed with flannel sheets and a down comforter. "Even during ninety-degree summers, it works. It's my perfect bedroom."

If you're not likely to manipulate your room's temperature,

though, stick with weights in top covers that match the conditions of your bedroom. Drafty rooms in cold climates might scream for down comforters or several cotton and woolen blankets topped by a bedcover or heavy quilt. Summers in the south might call for simple cotton bedspreads that are light and easy to pull up if the night air turns chilly.

Next, consider style, since the cover is usually what your eye directly falls upon when entering the room. After all, the bed is typically the focal point of every boudoir.

"The bed should have an invitational quality to it," says interior designer Judy Sheridan. "But you want to be practical, too. Ask yourself, when the bed is made, will it stay that way? Or are you apt to flop onto it with shoes on to watch TV?" She advises picking the type of covering to match how the bed is used. Patterns are typically more forgiving, she says. And cotton is more durable than a silk print.

Then, consider what mood you'd like the bed to convey. Will a soft cotton duvet in a pale blue and white stripes covering a feather comforter put you in the restive state you desire before drifting off to sleep? Or will a handmade quilt topping lavender and green sheets transform your room into an English cottage of tranquility as you stretch back at night to count your sheep. Or does a bold print in bright red and gold reaffirm, in your mind, that the bed is all about passion?

There is no right or wrong answer—the choice is yours to make. Just ask yourself if you want the bed to whisper relaxation. If so, stick to the cool, tranquil colors of blues and greens with a tone-on-tone scheme or a simple pattern.

On the other hand, if you wish your bed to arouse passion, then dress it in the colors of a fire: gold, red, copper, and go for bold and beautiful patterns and designs.

A PLACE TO LAY YOUR HEAD

A worthy pillow typically costs a fair amount of cash. Goose or duck down pillows are the softest and most cushy, which may or may not be your ideal. Feather-stuffed pillows offer a little more firmness, which helps prevent neck aches if you sleep on your side. Cotton or synthetic pillows are the most firm of all.

Olivia, thirty-one, from Berkeley, California, keeps an assortment of pillows on her bed with white washable covers ranging in size and softness as suits her mood—one oversized down, two standard pillows, and a small neck roll.

It's best to try out the store models for several minutes by mimicking sleep on them. Still, there's really no great way to test whether a pillow is right for you without trying it out for a full night. And since you can't return a used pillow, you may inadvertently build up a quite nice collection of guest pillows until you find The One.

Table Linens

Tablecloths, napkins, and placemats serve as excellent accent colors and textures in the dining nook of your nest. Not only are they extremely interchangeable for little cash, but they are a great way to fancy up your nest when events call for it. What's more, table linens are an excellent way to honor guests, according to the many women I interviewed.

"You rarely see cloth napkins anymore, even in restaurants," notes Isabelle, thirty-one, from Sacramento, California. "I think they are a nice finishing touch when having dinner guests."

Jasmine, twenty-nine, from Long Island, New York, also treats her guests to real linen napkins and placemats, even though she admits she eats at the couch most nights. "I hate paper stuff—it seems so wasteful and not as fun, cool, or colorful. Cloth napkins are cheap enough to use and lend an artistic flair."

Claire, thirty-five, from Bellingham, Washington, also always treats her guests to cloth, noting that "people like that because it makes them feel important enough to merit more than a paper towel."

Placemats are preferable to tablecloths, at least in my opinion, because they enable you to show off the table rather than hide it. Linen or raw-silk mats add gorgeous texture and color to the dining table and can easily be protected from spills and crumbs by placing a see-through vinyl mat atop them.

Cotton mats may be easier to care for, since you can toss them in the wash after a raucous dinner party where wine is freely poured. And plant-woven mats made of hemp or bamboo or sisal offers a naturalist touch of simplicity to the dinner table.

When it comes to colors and patterns, the table linens are one place where pretty much anything goes without risking color or pattern overload. Get as whimsical as you desire here—it only adds to the culinary experience. Or, keep it cool and simple for a more serene feast.

One common practice is to match your table linens with an accent color in your china or everyday dishware. This is one trick of pulling the dining table together. Another is using an accent color from a rug or curtains to tie in features of the entire room. Floral prints, geometric designs, organic patterns, and bold or soft colors— each lend a particular flair to the setting, presenting a visual appetizer of what's to come.

Now, if your dining table is one that has much to be desired (you're using your parents' old fold-out card table), a tablecloth is the route to go. In this case, a floor-length covering is optimal— don't leave half of the ugly metal fold-out legs showing if you can help it. And just like napkins or placemats, anything goes. Except paper—"fabric tablecloths are cheap if you look for them, and they make a big difference," says Lana, twenty-nine, from Los Angeles.

A bold design will draw attention to the drama of the dining table. Red-and-white checks lend a more casual, country air. White linen suggests a classic formality, one in which the textiles serve as a backdrop to the food, which you may or may not wish to emphasize, depending on your talents in the kitchen.

Throw Rugs

Rugs must have been one of the earliest textiles conceived for the home. If you lived in a cave, wouldn't you want something soft to sleep on instead of a cold, stony floor? Wouldn't you find a way to create a soft but substantial flooring for your newborn's first crawl? Or if home was a tent in the desert, wouldn't a smooth animal hide keep the sand gnats from nipping at your heels?

Nowadays, throw rugs are part decorative and part functional in most urban and suburban nests. You see them hung on walls for a splash of rich color and intricate designs, possibly doubling as a great soundproofing device for ultra-thin walls.

You also find them strategically placed around the rooms to define certain spaces—a rectangular Turkish rug bonds a sofa and two chairs together in an entertaining area; a sisal mat beneath a long wooden table makes it clear where the dining zone is.

Seasonal nesters lay out certain rugs only during particular times of the year (the sheepskin rug accompanies the hearth in winter, a smooth bamboo mat replaces it come spring). Others collect rugs of all types, layering their nest with a plush array of woven wool, cotton, and various plant-fiber rugs and mats, such as sisal, jute, even hemp.

When choosing throw rugs for your nest, let two questions dominate: How much traffic will this rug receive, and is it meant to visually define an area with its shape or color, or is its primary purpose to add warmth and cushioning to a hard, cold floor?

First, let's discuss traffic. In areas that receive ample foot traffic, be very careful about what type of rug, if any, you choose. Rugs in the entry area are most likely to get scrunched up from all the shuffling feet. Or pets. Reese, twenty-nine, from Cleveland, Ohio, can attest to this: "The big sisal rug that I put in the front entrance is constantly getting scrunched up because my two big dogs run to the front door to bark whenever anyone is walking by. Every five minutes, I have to fix the rug. So instead, I usually just keep it scrunched up most of the day."

Entry rugs are also prone to the most dirt and mud and rainwater of all rugs in the house, since this is where we stand when unloading before making our entrance into the rest of the nest. (Which is also why they are nice to have, so wooden floors don't receive the abuse.)

Interior designer Lauri Ward says that rugs in high-traffic areas are not the greatest idea. "Use a doormat outside the front door instead," she advises. That way, guests are encouraged to wipe their feet before entering. Or, as some cultures practice, even remove their shoes before walking indoors.

If you decide you must have an entry rug to define the space, choose it carefully. Pick a dark color at least, so it won't always look dingy as well as scrunched up, advises Leida, twenty-seven, from Seattle. "When we first moved in, my husband and his dad went to get a rug," she says. "They came home with a patterned rug with a cream background. We now live in Vermont with two dogs and it's brown. What were we thinking?"

In these areas—the front and back doors, below the sink, in front of the bath—only consider rugs that can be easily thrown in the wash—a cotton rag rug, for instance, in front of the sink, and a plush slide-proof bath mat in the bath. Above all, avoid rugs that are easily stained—sisal, for instance, begins to look pretty shoddy just from water spills, which in a rainy climate probably won't add sensual appeal to your nest.

To prevent slippage, you'll also want to use a nonskid rug pad or a simple rubber padding, which is available in most rug stores. Rug pads grip wood, concrete, or tile floors, keeping the rug in place. If you have a thick rug, you won't need to think about extra padding, but if your rug is paper thin, consider a pad that gives an extra half inch of cushion to your bare feet.

The second consideration in choosing a rug is its visual appeal. First, decide on the rug's ideal shape—is it meant to define a space within a large room? If so, you'll want the rug to be large enough to embrace all the pieces of furniture it is meant to tie together. For instance, you may want the dimensions to match the width of your sofa to tie it together with a coffee table and, say, two chairs.

Or, you may wish the rug to cover more of the room. A larger throw rug may embrace part of or the entire sofa, as well as the coffee table and two chairs atop it. Before purchasing, lay out newspapers in the dimensions of the rug you have in mind to get a visual of how its size and shape will affect the room and pieces of furniture within it.

Once you've determined the ideal size and shape (a round rug in front of bay windows may be the ideal shape to define a reading nook with armchair and lamp, for instance), consider colors and patterns.

If the room is already busy with patterns and designs, you may wish to downplay the throw rug and stick with a solid color or even a neutral—to give the other textiles in the room a chance to shine, rather than compete with the floor covering.

On the other hand, if your room lacks visual interest, consider a boldly patterned rug in rich colors—a rug that will define the color scheme of the room and dominate its palette. If you start your textile weaving with the rug, you can even use it to determine the color scheme of the room—choose a sofa covering or curtains using one or two colors from the rug. Pick an accent color from it for throw pillows or a lampshade as well.

Since rugs also offer a wonderful tactile sensuality to a room, a third consideration is its feel. Ask yourself how you'll be using the rug—to sink your feet into when you first get up in the morning on a cold winter day? If so, think plush and warm. Or, to give the bare feet a smooth, natural feel, as Sally, twenty-nine, from New York City, does with the straw rugs on her linoleum kitchen floor.

By the way, throw rugs needn't be expensive, unless you want the authentic, hand-tied Persian or Iranian rugs, which in my opinion are well worth the money, but not necessarily affordable for new nesters. Discount home retail shops have a decent selection of throw rugs to give you temporarily relief in the awful brown shag carpeting in your current rental. It's not a bad idea to experiment with these more replaceable rugs anyway before shelling out the big bucks, which you can do later on, after you've learned where you most love a rug (at the foot of your sofa or at the side of your bed, for instance) and what materials best suit your nesting needs.

Rug tiles with adhesive backs are a cheaper alternative to throw rugs, and offer great sensual appeal. Purchased in sets, these synthetic rug tiles come in many colors and patterns and can be placed in various arrangements around your nest—perfect for spaces where traditionally sized throw rugs won't fit. Because they stick directly to the floor, you also don't have that scrunching up problem in high-traffic areas.

Shower Curtains and Bath Mats

There are no set rules or guidelines here, except for one—these areas receive water splash, so you'll want to go with materials that are water resistant or that dry quickly. At a minimum, make sure you can throw it in the wash now and then for a quick pick-me-up.

Fun, whimsical, bold colors and patterns are great for bath mats and shower curtains—even in the tiniest of spaces. If, however, you're aiming for a spa-like experience in the bath, stick with the more restive patterns and palettes—the cooler shades of blue and purple and pale greens tend to have a more relaxing effect than, say, fire-engine red or sultry purple.

To protect the shower curtain, though, use a liner—either a see-through plastic number, so you can enjoy the curtain from either side, or one in a complementary color that adds a secondary layer of visual interest to the room.

Bath towels are yet a third way to add textile interest to the bathroom. The sensual nester, naturally, needs the most plush bath towels she can afford.

And don't forget hand towels by the sink—especially if you like to entertain. As Claire, thirty-five, from Bellingham, Washington, puts it: "Puuleeeeaase put out a clean and obvious guest hand towel for God's sake when entertaining. One thing that drives me crazy is when you go to the bathroom in someone's house and the only towel to dry your hands on is the same one they use to wipe themselves with!"

Roomie Advice

If you find a textile you love, but must get approval from a roommate or lover, consider using the fail-proof tactic of Jasmine, twenty-nine, from Long Island, New York: "Call with your cell phone and say, 'I found great curtains, what style do you want?' On the spot, he [or she] won't argue, so when you come home and put them up, he [or she] will probably love them."

Seasonal Décor

First things first, I'm hardly suggesting that you change the look and feel of your nest four times a year. It's hard enough to get just basic decorating down. But once the colors of your walls have been painted and your basic textiles have been chosen, you might enjoy changing a few fabrics in your nest every once in a while—throw pillows and blankets, your bedding, even a rug or the curtains.

"Seasonal decorating gives your home a fresh feel," says interior designer Lauri Ward. "People in their twenties and thirties usually don't have second homes, so rotating accessories and fabrics is a great way to have fun with your home. It gets boring to have the same look year round."

Swapping a sisal floor mat in the summer for a wool rug in the winter, for instance, can really cozy up a room. Switching the dark gray slipcovers on your sofa during the cold months for a white canvas covering in the summer, refreshes and lightens up the look and feel of your main entertaining area.

Something as simple as using soft green linens in the dining room during spring instead of the rich reds you opt for during the winter can give your nest the uplift we often crave when the seasons change.

Hannah, thirty-four, from Van Nuys, California, for instance, has two sets of café curtains (the type that cover just the lower section of a window, allowing privacy and light into the room) in her kitchen. One is a rich red-and-taupe stripe for fall and winter. The other is a zingy retro sunflower and lime-green pattern for spring and summer.

To add to the seasonal décor in her kitchen, she fills a ceramic bowl with Indian corn and small pumpkins in the fall, and then keeps a stock of green apples and lemons in the same bowl during the springtime.

Ethel, thirty-nine, from Philadelphia, changes the color scheme in her nest each season. On her tan couch, she'll change the color of the decorative pillows, the throw on the back of a chair, slipcovers on chairs, and even the ornaments around the room. She makes the switch on one of her cleaning days as a form of motivation—she looks forward to the uplift and considers it a reward for seasonal cleaning.

Veronica, twenty-eight, from Los Angeles, also changes little textiles around her nest—placemats, linens, pillow covers—depending on the season. "I have a lot of pillows from Pottery Barn, and they're always coming out with new covers, so it's a fun way to transition between seasons," she says.

Seasonal decorating isn't just about changing the look of your nest—it can also be a great way to extend the life of your textiles and prepare your nest appropriately for the seasons. "If you have two sets of slipcovers," says Ward, "you'll preserve each of them longer, since you're only using them six months of the year."

Likewise, alternating curtains helps you maintain the upkeep of the fabrics as well as use the most suitable window covering for the time of year. Heavy velvet curtains in the winter will insulate your home better than, say, thin white linen or cotton drapes. Alternating curtains also gives you a good opportunity to clean these fabrics once a year, which helps preserve their lifespan.

Changing your bedding during summer and winter is another practical move that refreshes your bedroom and extends the life of your bedding. Isabelle, thirty-one, from Sacramento, California, for instance, swaps her lighter covers in the summer for a down comforter and a dark-colored duvet cover each winter.

Brice, twenty-six, from Chicago, also switches her lighter quilt to a heavier one come winter. After all, seasonal décor, especially when it comes to textiles in the nest, will keep you nest sensual to the seasons no matter what time of year it is.

7

Floors

The Northern Oriole blankets the floor of its hanging nest with cottony plant fibers, wool, and hair, creating a cozy carpet for its chicks.

 We walk on them. We pace them. We lie on them. And on occasion, I admit, we sometimes do nothing but stare at them all day. While the bottom-most layer of our nest may seem an unlikely aspect to improve upon without major renovation work, there are many things we can do to heighten the sensuality of our floors. Which isn't a bad idea. Second to the walls of a room, the floors have the most surface area, and therefore, are dramatic contributions to our living space, like it or not.

If you are renting, there may be limited alterations you are allowed to make to your floors. Still, whatever you are dealt in the luck of apartment dwellings, there are many ways to make your floors look more sensual that they currently are. Then again, I don't know a single landlord who would object to your refinishing hardwood floors yourself—assuming you have the competence to do so—or replacing the 700-square-foot shag carpeting in your studio with a sophisticated medium plush Berber in light gray. And whose feathers could possibly be ruffled if you ripped out the torn vinyl tiles in your bathroom and replaced them with a shiny mod linoleum print? If you're lucky, the landlord may even be willing to split the cost— but no promises here. After all, refurbished flooring adds value to the property.

Assuming you have the will and means to put in a new floor for your nest, there are a few general concepts to keep in mind: Bold colors and designs will overwhelm a small space, so if your kitchen is a four-by-six-foot walk-in closet, don't go for Marimekko-print linoleum tiles in bold orange flowers. Consider a minimalist pattern or a plain, muted color instead.

Also, keep in mind that light colors will increase the sense of space—oak floors finished in a light amber stain or simply sealed with a clear polyurethane varnish appear more expansive than oak floors stained in dark mahogany. Dark floors, on the other hand, give a more formal, stately feeling. They serve as great backdrops to the furniture on the floor, and in large rooms, they can make an expansive space more intimate.

The most important part of putting in a new floor for your nest, however, is to try out what you have in mind. Don't be in a hurry to make a decision. Lay samples of the wood or tile or linoleum on the existing floor for at least a week, moving them around during different times of the day to get the full effect of how your new floor will look with changes in light during the day and when lit artificially at night.

Let's talk specifics for those of you ready to hit the floor running, so to speak.

hardwood

Hardwood floors top the list of my sensual aesthetics for the home. Cool to the feet on hot summer days, warm in the winter when exposed to midday sun. Rich in color, from amber to mahogany, and ripe with texture from the grain of the wood. The sound of wooden heels stepping on creaky planks. The scent of Murphy oil drifting through the room after an annual spring-cleaning.

And then there are all the variations in wood floor—large planks that hearken back to colonial days, the ubiquitous red oak thin strips, and various patterns of parquet wooden tiles adding a pleasing geometry and dimension to the room.

If your nest is lucky enough to have hardwood floors, it's important to take care of them properly. For starters, sweep or vacuum your floors every week or even more often if you tend to track in a lot of dirt, grease, or grime. (To avoid this, though, establish a no-shoe policy in your nest, and stick to it—you'll have to do a lot less cleaning.) If you fail to clean regularly, you'll grind the dirt and dust into your floor finish, which will eventually dull it. Unless you're going for the rustic look, this won't add charm to your nest.

In addition to sweeping the dirt and dust away, you'll want to occasionally clean your hardwood floors with a mild detergent or floor cleaner. Since hardwood floors all have different finishes—modern floors are typically finished with polyurethane, but older floors may be sealed with an aging lacquer or shellac or simply with floor wax—you'll want to experiment with the best cleaning solution for your particular floor.

Older finishes may simply need to be topped off with a fresh coat of floor paste wax. Newer polyurethane finished floors, on the other hand, should not be waxed, and are best cleaned with a damp (never soaking wet) sponge mop, using a floor cleaning solution or a home-prepared mixture of water and mild dishwashing or laundry detergent. What you're aiming for after a cleaning is that glistening shine and no obvious dirt or grease marks on the surface. You may need to experiment with different cleaning products and tools until you find the combination that makes your unique hardwood floors shine.

Occasionally, you may even wish to rent a buffer and polish your floors. Not only does buffing the floors really bring out the beauty of the wood, but it's also a great way to help maintain the finish—especially for floors that have seen years and years of abuse, such as claws of pets, toys of children, heels of divas, and scratches from chair legs near the dining room table.

For hardwood floors in dire need of repair, you might consider the laborious task of refinishing them. Refinishing floors is one of the most intense home improvement jobs you'll ever undertake (I'm writing this from experience), but newly refinished floors can really improve the sensuality of your nest. Especially if you have a large open floor plan, because your eye can't help but be influenced by the floor when you walk into the room.

Our dark oak floors had been abused by several previous patch-up jobs with mismatched stains and scratches galore when we decided to refinish them to a lighter cherry color, eliminating the scratches and weird swirls of stain that existed on parts of the floor. This warmed up the entire feel of our nest, since the lighter color reflected more light into the room and eliminated that cold, dark feeling of our former floors.

While our floors still have gouges here and there (they are more than eighty years old, after all), they exude a warmth and sensual appeal now that they are restored. It was well worth the hellish two weekends it took us to do both levels of our two-story home.

If you have plans to refinish your floors (and if I could do it without any technical or craftsmanship skills to boast of, so can you), it's best to get a book on the topic—or at least have a long discussion with someone who has done the job recently and can walk you through all the steps. However, I'll lay out briefly what is involved to give you an idea of what you're in for.

The first step is to rent the heavy, impossible machinery you'll need to refinish your floors—a drum sander (which looks like a cross between a lawn mower and an industrial vacuum), an edger (which is a heavy disc sander that my husband and I nicknamed "the back-breaker"), three grades of sandpaper for both (36, 60, and 100 grit), a hand scraper, and materials for staining and sealing the wood, which include a long-handled lamb's wool applicator, stain, poly-urethane sealer, a tray for pouring the stain and finish, tack cloth, and a large sanding block with 100-grit sandpaper for lifting the grain between coats of sealer.

The second step is to remove the old finish and prepare the wood floors for a new stain or simply a clear sealer. You'll first use the giant sander machine and "mow" your floor with a coarse grit (36) sand-paper, sanding in the direction of the wood or on the diagonal at first, followed by a second pass on the grain. Overlap as you go, being careful not to gouge the wood along the way. This, by the way, was the most satisfying part of the process for me, because you'll in-stantly see virgin wood break through the old stain as you sand.

Once you've done your first pass in the heaviest grid sandpaper, you take the edger, kneeling on your knees, and do the same at the edges of the wall where the giant sander couldn't reach. If you don't have lower back problems before you attempt this, you likely will afterward.

After sanding the edges, you'll need a paint scraper to get the old stain out of the corners (another fun job!). At this point your room will be covered in sawdust and old stain. We rented a shop vacuum to help with the cleanup—the suction is far superior to a regular home vacuum, and with a rental, you won't have to then worry about cleaning your vacuum up from all the stain and sealer residue that's inevitably left behind.

Then, you're ready for the second pass, repeating the whole process, using 60-grit sandpaper. Once that's done, along with a second cleanup, you'll do one more pass using 100 grit, which leaves the wood smooth and ready to accept the stain or just the sealer if you're now in love with the light, fresh wood that's now gracing your floors. (We almost skipped the stain after sanding the floors because we couldn't bear the idea of putting a new color atop this pristine wood. But we did, and now we're glad because the cherry tone is so inviting and warm.)

After a thorough cleaning with a rag doused with mineral spirits, let the floor dry, then lightly wipe it down with a tack cloth to remove any remaining debris, dust or lint—be sure to wear clean socks during this process so you won't leave shoe marks or oil from the bottoms of your feet. Then, you're ready to stain or simply seal the wood.

Always test the color before going crazy with it, no matter how eager you are to get the job done—it's a four-day process at a minimum, so plan ahead and don't be in a hurry. We tested several stain colors on a scrap piece of red oak we got from a lumberyard. Then, we practiced in the closet before we hit the main rooms, applying the stain in long sweeping motions using a lamb's wool applicator attached to an extension pole for the main area and a paintbrush along the edges.

Staining was a two-person job. I applied, and my husband followed after me on hands and knees with a bucket of clean rags to wipe up the excess so the stain dried evenly and the color looked uniform.

Once the stain dries (give it a good twenty-four hours or however long the directions on the product says to wait), you'll apply your first coat of sealer, typically a polyurethane varnish. There are different levels of gloss on these sealers—if you're going for a natural look, stick with the antique or flat finishes. The higher satin or gloss finishes will give your floor more shine, a more polished look, which may or may not be ideal, since high-gloss finishes tend to show dirt and blemishes more readily. Most nesters go for a medium-gloss finish.

Sealer comes in quick-dry versions, but it's not a bad idea to wait twenty-four hours after the first application. You'll want to do at least two more coats after the first, sanding and cleaning with mineral spirits and a tack cloth between each application. Three coats of sealer will provide a durable, hard finish for your floors that most lifestyles will have a hard time wearing down.

One note of caution: Always map out how you will start and finish the application of your stain and sealer. You will need to end up near a door. And make sure that door isn't locked from the outside! When my husband refinished our downstairs floors (I conveniently left that weekend for a trip down south), he polyurethaned himself into a corner because his escape route—the front door—was locked and the key we normally keep in the keyhole wasn't there. Luckily there was a window right there, and he was able to crawl out. Otherwise, all of his hard labor would have been ruined by footsteps across the polyurethane finish.

If this process sounds ridiculously insane to do on your own (and paying someone else to do it can cost a pretty penny), you may want to consider painting your scratched-up wooden floors instead. It's a practice that was common in Victorian homes, and I've seen some gorgeous examples of wooden floors painted Chinese red, pale green, even in pickled white glaze—all of which added visual interest to the room.

Keep in mind, unless you use a light glaze instead of paint, you won't see the grain of the wood like you would with a stain. That's one reason why painting a floor might be the preferred method of upgrading a wood floor, because it will mask flaws more than a stain.

Zoe, thirty-three, from Dallas, has seen one wooden floor in a bad polish repainted in black, then finished in a high-gloss shellac and buffed, which she recalls, "hid the major flaws and looked completely different and cool."

If your floor previously has a finish on it, you'll need to remove it per steps mentioned above or the paint won't adhere to the wood. Otherwise, a thorough cleaning and drying out will suffice.

Oil-based paint will give you a longer lifespan than water-based paint, since it tends to be more durable. But paint stores may also carry paints made specifically for floors or for outdoor use, meaning that it will hold up in the harshest of conditions, such as muddy wet rain boots and metal-tipped cowboy boots.

If you decide to paint the entire floor one color, you'll simply apply it with a roller as you would were you painting a wall, first cutting in at the edges with a brush. For a long life, consider at least two coats—three to be safe.

Patterns, such as black-and-white checks or green-and-yellow harlequin diamonds, or stenciled designs require a little more planning, measuring out the pattern, then laying it out with masking tape.

Regardless of whether you pick a solid color or a pattern or even decide to stencil designs in a border around your floor, you'll want to top off the painted floor with a sealer to preserve its life. For floors that receive a lot of use—kitchens, front entryways, and bathrooms, top it off with two or even three coats of epoxy-based sealer. As with sealing wood, you may choose between a variety of glosses, from antique or matte finish to one that shines like lacquer.

tile, stone, or brick

While they may feel cool and hard on the feet and not offer much in the way of sound absorption, the look and feel of ceramic tile, stone, or brick floors offer three very distinct variations of sensuality to a nest floor.

Polished so smoothly you can count the pores on your face when staring into them, or laid unsealed with a texture so rough your manicurist might never again need to break out the wax paraffin, these flooring options are manufactured in so many different variations, you can get just about any look or feel you desire for your nest when using them. Laying tile, brick, or stone in untraditional places, like the living or bedroom, can even add some interesting contrast and surprise to your nest.

Traditional ceramic tiles are made of clay and come in a variety of sizes—from large terra-cotta squares to tiny mosaic-sized cubes; their earthy, human-scaled quality adds a degree of craftsmanship and individuality to the nest. Whether glazed, unglazed to reveal their natural color and texture, or hand painted, tiles offer up a bit of geometric interest to the floor of your nest. They also provide a tactile sensuality, especially in warm climates, since they tend to always feel cool on the feet. The grout between the tiles adds its own decorative element and flair, since you may choose from an endless range of spacing widths and colors.

Stone, which comes in tile or slab form, is made of a variety of types of stone, from marble to granite to limestone. Installed similarly to tile using grout, they offer their own degree of sensuality to a room—irregular slabs of slate, for instance, gives a sense of expansiveness to a room, not unlike a garden room in a castle somewhere far away. White marble square tiles, on the other hand, have an air of classical elegance in, say, a spacious bathroom. Highly polished granite tiles might be the exact bedroom flooring you've always dreamed of to showcase your collection of sheepskin rugs thrown beside the bed.

Like tile, stone flooring offers geometric interest to the eye as well as a cool, clean touch to bare feet. Walking across a stone floor offers great sensual sounds whether your feet are bare or sporting the sexiest kitten shoes in your closet (click, click, click). There are no creaks with a stone floor as there are with hardwood, but echoes tend to be louder in such rooms, which may be what you're after, for instance, if you love the grandiose sound of echoes in an entry hallway. Otherwise, throw rugs help absorb sounds if they're bothersome.

A brick floor adds an element of earthiness to the nest. The gorgeous color and indoor/outdoor sensuality of a brick floor can cozy up a kitchen, entertaining area, even a bedroom. That's why little Italian restaurants in Manhattan with brick-laid patios feel so warm and human in scale. They offer a natural richness in color and texture to any space.

The benefits of ceramic-tile, stone, or brick flooring are many— if sealed properly, they are easy to clean and perfect for areas that are prone to water spills, such as the kitchen, bathroom, or a sunroom filled with potted plants. Ceramic and stone floors tend to give an old-world flavor to the nest, while brick flooring adds a little bit of provincial living to an urban or suburban nest.

The drawbacks? While tiles, stone, and brick are easy to keep clean and are great for resisting water if they are sealed, the grout between the pieces is hard to keep fresh and new, so that is a consideration if you're not a diligent housekeeper. Also, while these are, in general, durable surfaces, they are not impervious to chipping, so if your nest is prone to disasters from small animals, children, or care-

less guests who scuttle around in their cycling cleats, a sturdier resilient floor may be the preferred choice.

When choosing a type of tile, stone, or brick, keep the following
in mind—you want the color and scale to match the architecture of
the space. Carissa, thirty-five, from Chicago, who recently retiled
two powder rooms in her nest with her father-in-law's help, says
picking tile is daunting.

"You've got to bring samples home, stick them in the room, and
try to match them with paint or wallpaper," she says. She ended up
with a tumbled marble-style yellow tile with rust-colored grout.
"Sounds gross," she admits, "but it looks pretty swanky."

Nita, thirty, from Los Angeles, advises laying out a number of
tiles in your top pick before purchasing the entire amount you need.
"One tile looks different than an entire kitchen filled with them,"
she says.

Large tiles with bold colors, such as a highly polished granite, can
easily overwhelm a tiny cottage kitchen, which may find a better
flooring match in brick, tiny glass mosaic tiles, or simple white tiles
made of marble or ceramic. On the other hand, a giant kitchen/din-
ing room with an open floor plan that, say, incorporates a wood-

burning stove in the corner (a girl can fantasize) can most likely handle the gravity of large, irregular, roughened slate slabs, which would match the grand open space and offer the durable flooring that preparing food, eating, and tending to the hearth demands.

The pattern in which tiles are laid adds to their visual contribution—the traditional grid approach gives a sense of order and uniformity to a room, whereas a diagonal layout may jazz up an otherwise boring rectilinear space. Grout width and color is another way to enhance a tile or stone floor. Using different colors of tiles or setting them in a distinct pattern may also spice up a traditional tile layout.

Before you lay tile, brick, or stone slabs, you'll need to make sure your subflooring is properly prepared and strong enough to hold up the type of tile, stone, or brick flooring you choose to install. Since these are heavier materials than wood, linoleum, or carpeting, the foundation needs to be sturdy. I recommend professional inspection and assistance.

Otherwise, laying the tiles, slabs, or brickwork is a manageable job to do on your own, assuming you have time, because laying this type of flooring requires a commitment of several days' hard manual labor, the proper tools and supplies, and above all, meticulous planning.

I'd advise you to get a how-to book on tiling and read carefully before you commit to the job (see the end of this book for further reading resources). Or, take a class at the Home Depot or an adult education–type course. As with refinishing hardwood floors, the more prepared you are to do the job, the better the end result.

To give you an idea of what's involved, here is the basic process. The first step is to inspect the subfloor by removing the existing tiles or hardwood or resilient flooring (but beware that resilient flooring made prior to the 1980s may contain asbestos and in that case should be removed by a professional only). The subfloor (ideally concrete but wood works, too) will need to be repaired of any deterioration or unevenness or any other defect that could affect the laying of the tiles.

While tiles can be laid directly upon a roughened concrete floor, a wood subfloor needs additional support by covering it with two layers of plywood—first an underlayment grade, which is the stronger layer, then a tile-backing grade, both of which can be purchased at hardware or home-improvement stores.

Next, you'll want to determine the layout of your tiles by measuring them and establishing placement along the main axis of the room, using plastic spacers to separate the tiles for the grout. Experiment with placement and grout widths until you've determined a layout that works with the space, then mark the layout with chalk lines. You may need to precut some tiles to fit the space.

After applying the adhesive to the tile-backing plywood, you'll lay down the tiles in rows, using plastic spacers between each one. As you nestle each tile into place, use a trowel and clean rags to wipe up excess adhesive that may ooze up over the sides. When in place, hammer the tiles into the adhesive, protecting them with a padded board.

Once the tiles are in place, remove the spacers and prepare the grout, which is then pored over the tiles, a small section at a time, and packed tightly into the joints, wiping away the excess as you go.

Tile and brick floors usually need to be sealed to avoid stains and superficial scratches. Wait several weeks after laying the tile, and then seal the floor with a large brush or roller. Keep them clean by regular sweeping and mopping with a mild detergent when needed.

resilient floors

Composed of linoleum, vinyl, rubber, cork, or a combination of the above mixed with petroleum derivatives, resilient sheet flooring or tiles are manufactured floor coverings made to look like the real thing—stone, wood, tile. They are lighter in weight and cost less than the materials they emulate, and they are easier to install, making them perfectly fine nesting material for the nonpurist nester.

While the purist may associate resilient floors with public places (since rubber tiles, sheets of linoleum, and laminates are often the preferred choice in flooring for restaurant kitchens, dorm bathrooms, and gym locker rooms), don't automatically write them off if the ratty linoleum in your bathroom is begging for a replacement—especially if you live in an apartment, where your residence is only temporary. A new resilient floor is easier on the pocket than, say, Mexican terracotta tiles. And flooring is one thing you can't take with you.

"There are some absolutely wonderful new vinyl peel-and-stick tiles out there that look like real ceramic and slate," says Kasey, twenty-five, from Hoboken, New Jersey. "They are beautiful and incredibly easy to install. They can transform a room in one afternoon. New laminates instead of traditional hardwood floors can even fool professionals," she says.

Linoleum, which is made of ground cork, resins, and wood, among other naturally occurring substances, is perhaps the best-known form of resilient floor. Developed in the mid-1800s, it even has a flair of authentic retro-ism, since many turn-of-the-century houses used this material in high-traffic areas, such as laundry rooms and kitchens.

Sold in sheets up to twelve feet wide, which means you may not have any seams if covering a tiny floor, linoleum is attached by an adhesive or in some cases, just left to float atop the subfloor. It's also available in tiles, which are much easier to install than their ceramic sisters, since some even come with a self-adhering backing.

Go-Girl Guidance

"The trick to linoleum is purchasing the 'end of roll' remnant. It'll only work for small spaces, but 'end of roll' is usually discounted, which allows you to choose a groovy linoleum you otherwise wouldn't be able to afford."

—*Zoe, thirty-three, from Dallas*

Vinyl, which was developed during the middle half of the twentieth century, is another common home choice for resilient floors. Often, you'll find more choice in colors and patterns in vinyl versus linoleum. However, vinyl tiles or sheets are typically harder on the soles than linoleum, which may be a drawback if you wish to use it in areas that require long periods of standing, like in the kitchen where you cook and do dishes, or the laundry zone, where you iron and fold clothing.

Laminate, which was developed more recently, does a particularly good job at imitating wood, stone, and tile. But, again, if you are a purist, it pays to save up for the real thing. While I'm not a stickler for details, even I can tell the difference between a wood floor and a laminate floor that mimics parquet. (And the laminate version always looks slightly cheap to me.)

Likewise, if you're going for maximum sensuality in your nest, laminate floors that look like wood, and won't feel like wood on the feet. Nor will they sound like wood when you walk across them barefoot or in leather slippers. The slap of barefoot and the shuffle of slipper is missing or muted at best. If such details are important to you, save up for the real thing. On the other hand, if noise reduction and draft insulation are critical factors in choosing your flooring, you may actually prefer laminate or other resilient flooring, since it tends to offer more absorption of sound and updrafts.

The process of installing resilient floor sheets involves measuring the space, then determining where, if any, the seams should lie. Then the sheets are cut using a straightedge for a rough fit. Fastening the sheet(s) to the floor depends on the type of flooring used, but either you'll have a self-adhesive backing or you'll apply an adhesive and roll the flooring across the room. Once it has set, you can trim the edges. If you're simply floating the sheet on the floor, you'll lay it out, weight it down then trim off the excess at the walls and corners.

Laying resilient tiles, on the other hand, requires more planning— especially if you're aiming for a grid pattern. However, because they are flexible and easier to cut than tile, they are far easier to install than ceramic or stone tiles. You'll want to mark out the pattern and apply adhesive, but you won't need to worry about grout line spacing, because resilient tiles lack grout lines.

The planning and layout will be the same as with ceramic or stone tiles—even flexible tiles must follow a straight line or your black-and-white checkerboard floor will look like it's been hit by Hurricane Ivan. The nice thing about resilient tiles, though, is that you can walk on them as soon as you lay them. In a teeny room, it could even be a one-day affair.

As with tile and wood floors, resilient floors require regular sweeping or vacuuming and frequent cleaning with a mild detergent. Some types of resilient floors require occasional waxing for a finished, polished look, but not all do, so check with the manufacturer before you break out the floor wax. Overpolishing can lead to a dulled surface.

carpet

I'm not a huge fan of carpet ever since I saw a program on public television back in the 1980s about all the microscopic organisms, dust mites, and other unmentionables that burrow deep in the pile. I've also read that carpets can trigger allergies and aggravate asthma.

🐦 Go-Girl Guidance 🐦

"Carpet seems like a good idea, but it isn't healthy for you and it's more difficult to clean than hard surfaces. Especially if you're worried about lead paint dust in your house, you want something that's easy to clean."

—*Kate, twenty-nine, from Grand Rapids, Michigan*

Still, there is an undeniable world of sensuality buried in the fibers of thick, plush carpeting. Carpet is luxurious on the tootsies. You can bury your toes in it while reading Chaucer. When you step out of your bed in the morning, your feet don't turn numb from the cold. A carpeted room is a quiet, warm space. Assuming you choose a relatively dark color, keeping one clean is simply a matter of regular vacuuming and vigilance regarding spills.

Picking the type of carpet is best done at a carpet distributor or retailer, since you'll want to feel for softness, thickness, and durability. Natural carpets are made of wool, cotton, or a blend of natural fibers. Synthetic carpets usually boast a large percentage of nylon or polyester. Many are now manufactured with a combination of wool and nylon, creating a soft, strong carpet that feels natural but also has the easy-cleaning properties of synthetics.

As for color, always err on the side of gray. So warns Kira, twenty-six, from Seattle. When she and her husband first moved into their house, they tore up some flooring and replaced it with cream carpet. "It looked absolutely fabulous until we got a puppy a few months later," she says. "Next time, I'm going darker."

Installation is best left to the professionals, since making seams requires heavy equipment that isn't readily available. If your current nest hosts a shag or two, consider shampooing it once a year to keep the dust out and the plush as fresh as possible.

concrete

Concrete floors, often the bane of basement apartments, are not necessarily the bane of nesting. You can polish a concrete floor so that it is as smooth and shiny as marble, giving your nest a modern industrial look and feel. Or you can sandblast the concrete, creating an interesting texture for a more rustic nesting floor. You can also paint a concrete floor and finish it with a high-gloss shellac or a flat polyurethane sealer.

Because of its strength, concrete floors make excellent subfloors for other types of flooring, such as tile or slate, so if you can't live with the cold, unimpressive surface, you're at least halfway there to slabs of slate or tile.

Improvements start by patching up any cracks or blemishes in the concrete using mortar manufactured specifically for the job. If you wish to sandblast or polish, a professional is worth hiring, since the equipment alone might cost you an arm and leg.

To stain or paint, you'll want to clean and dry the concrete floor, and then prepare it so that it is more accepting by coating it with a solution of water and muriatic acid, available at most paint or hardware stores. Once that has thoroughly dried, you may stain or paint the floor as you would a wooden floor, with checks or designs or simply a solid color. Ask your paint store about using a stain or paint specifically manufactured for concrete—this may help preserve its lifespan. To prevent chips or fading, top the color with a layer of clear polyurethane sealer, either in a flat, antique finish for a more subtle look, or a high-gloss finish for an eye-popping effect.

Since the echo in rooms with concrete floors is almost too loud to bear and they are always ice cold no matter what the weather is like outside, throw rugs are essential for nesting. Be sure to have several on hand—cozy wool rugs and sheepskins in winter, jute mats or white cotton canvas throws during warmer weather.

Lighting

Whip-poor-wills use light and shadow filtering through trees to camouflage their eggs laid on a simple bed of leaves.

 Walk into any chic bistro at night and you'll instantly receive a lesson in lighting. Indirect lighting, ambient lighting, accent lighting—these are the essence of sensual dining. And sensual living. Manipulating the light in your nest not only enables you to evoke a specific mood but also to heighten the senses.

Sensual lighting is a critical component to taking the edge off urban and suburban dwelling (since there is no edge to country living that I am aware of). Think about it: Could there be a calmer image than a reading lamp atop a table next to an overstuffed armchair? Or a few artfully arranged candles set atop a dining-room table? Or even a single spotlight casting a pool of shadows on the wall behind a leafy plant?

Accent lighting highlights the good, and distracts from the bad. Tinted lights can make or break a complexion, while task lighting can make or break the end result of an art project or the elegance of, say, a knitted scarf.

Light creates drama and movement around the nest, designating certain spaces for certain tasks and other areas for visual pause, creating a hierarchy of importance for all of your belongings.

how to light a room

One word: layers. Creating a sensual space with light requires several sources of light, each yielding its own pool, stream, or glow in the critical corners of your nest, the layers weaving in and out of each other, creating depth, drama, and mystery. The source of this light should never come from a standard 100-watt overhead bulb. Different wattage, colors, and angles of light spread carefully around a room all contribute to the ambiance of the nest. Let's break down the layers, shall we?

Task Lighting

Decorators may differ in their opinions on how to light a room, but most agree that the first step is to determine what tasks around the nest require direct lighting so you can actually see what you're doing—plucking your eyebrows, chopping broccoli, needlepointing a Christmas stocking.

Take the nesting ritual of reading the morning paper. Where do you normally conduct this daily rite? If the answer is your dining nook in the kitchen, which is beside a window that receives generous morning light, you are in luck and you only need to think about how to maximize that natural source of light while preserving the privacy needed for perusing headlines in a nightgown. (Hint: Voile curtains or sheer shades offer just enough privacy for lazy mornings.)

If natural light is a joke in your breakfast nook, then you will need a pendant light hung over your table, directing light onto your paper. Ideally, the light will shine directly from above or at a slight angle from the side, so the light hits your paper and perhaps a breakfast bowl of fruit and yogurt, but doesn't cast a glare into your eyes or create shadows from your head as you pour over the latest scandals of local politics.

Next, consider the tasks involved in preparing a meal. You'll need strong direct light on the countertops where you read recipes and cube tofu, and you'll want additional direct lighting on the range and sink areas, where you wash dishes, stir, and wait for the pot to boil.

Track or cable lighting is ideal for the kitchen, since you can aim several beams of light onto different areas. If you love the effect, but aren't crazy about the look, consider low-voltage track lights, which have very tiny cans and are not too noticeable if you pick white tracks on a white ceiling or if you choose a style that's wiry and minimalist.

In the bedroom, task lighting becomes critical next to the bed if you read to fall asleep or (shame on you!) bring your laptop into the sheets to finish up some work. You'll want a low-aimed source of strong light here—a table lamp with a wide-brimmed, bell-shaped shade will splash plenty of direct light onto the pages of your book, but not in your eyes, keeping the rest of the room calm and cozy for co-sleepers. An over-the-shoulder wall-mounted lamp also throws good reading light onto a book or magazine without creating an annoying glare in your eyes.

Task lighting around a bedroom mirror may also be necessary if you tend to do your primary grooming there. For best results, place two sources of light on either side of the mirror. This casts an even glow around your face, eliminating ugly shadows that you get from direct overhead lighting. (The ugly overhead lighted look, by the way, explains why you always look horrendous when you get your hair cut—the overhead recessed lighting is great and necessary task lighting for your stylist, but it usually doesn't do a girl's complexion any favors.)

The bathroom, of course, will need similar task lighting treatment around the mirror where you extract blemishes and apply makeup and where other nesters may shave their faces. If you tend to read in the bathtub, you'll also want to consider a direct light source above or to the side of your tub, so you won't develop eyestrain in the one place in your nest that is meant to be most relaxing.

Once you've established all the direct lighting for the various tasks around your nest, you may move on to the second layer.

Accent Lighting

In this layer, your goal is to direct soft beams of light to the parts of your nest that you wish to draw attention to—a beloved piece of art, a wooden sculpture, an earthy brick wall that serves a gorgeous textured backdrop to an indoor garden, bold redwood ceiling beams that might otherwise get lost in the dark. Doing so inadvertently places the areas you are less keen to show off—the cracked plaster on the western wall, for instance—in the dark.

It is the accent lighting that creates motion and drama in the room, leading the eye from one lit corner to another, and telling the gaze where to get excited and where to take pause. Accent lighting keeps the eye moving around the room, giving a space motion and sensual appeal at a far higher voltage than a single overhead light, which establishes no hierarchy of importance to your belongings.

Accent lighting not only draws the eye to the more dramatic aspects of a room when you walk in, but can also be used to mask its faults. A low ceiling, for instance, may feel oppressive, but if you direct light upward using an uplight wall sconce or a torch table or floor lamp, your gaze will naturally be drawn toward the sky, expanding that sense of ceiling height and even diverting the eye away from a poorly patched plaster wall underneath.

Accent lighting beamed onto a painting or sculpture highlights its importance in the room, creating a hierarchy of visual drama, since the eye naturally falls onto well-lit areas. For best results, spotlight artwork from above or below at a thirty-degree angle. For sculpture, minimize or enhance the play of shadows by experimenting with various types of spotlighting. Aim two spotlights from either side of the piece, and you'll balance light with shadow. Focus one strong beam on a sculpture from above and you'll exaggerate the shadow, which may be the point.

Washing or "grazing" a textured wall with a beam of light that skims the surface, such as you might find with uplight cans placed on the floor along a brick wall, brings out its rough texture, creating art in and of itself.

You can also use accent lighting to manipulate the size of a room: In a small room, washing a wall with light will expand the space. Graze the short walls in a galley-shaped room, and those surfaces will seem to have widened, because the light enhances their size and scale. To transform a giant studio into a more intimate, cozy space, place small pools of light in several parts of the space—a tree lamp, which directs light upward and downward, in the entertaining area; wall sconces near the dining zone; a small table lamp by the bed.

Backlighting an indoor tree by aiming a beam onto the wall behind it, causing the light to reflect back onto the backside of its leaves, or silhouetting the plant with uplight cans placed on the floor behind it, casting light up onto its branches and shadowing its front, not only creates drama in a room but also casts a chorus of shadows onto the walls. Turn on a ceiling fan or keep the window open on a breezy night, and watch these shadows dance across the room, adding movement to the sensual offerings of your nest.

Ambient Lighting

The final layer of lighting is what creates the overall mood in a room, the ambiance. To perfect this layer, one must take in the entire room's offerings of light during the day and evening and make adjustments in the areas that either exhibit too much glare or not enough glow at all.

Ambient lighting takes into account the sum of all light in a room and ensures that one half of the space does not radiate like the midday sun while the other half sulks in cool, dank darkness. Effective ambient lighting also takes into account that all the light sources in a room come from various types of light: a sixty-watt rose-tinted bulb here, a flame of a candle there, a sharply focused full-spectrum halogen beam on the portrait of Grandma Ruby in her flapper days.

Let's go back to those bistros I mentioned at the beginning of the chapter. Tiny tables are often lit by unobtrusive glass pendants hung delicately over each table, providing the only task lighting patrons need to make their dinner choices. Accent lights highlight wall art using spidery but delicate cables and tightly focused halogen bulbs. Uplights uplift the ceilings and expand the brick walls they graze. Candles add to the ambiance, along with carefully positioned mirrors that reflect the room's overall glow, creating the moody, dramatic, and calm spaces to slow down and savor.

All of these light sources work together to create the ambiance, and no lighting task is complete until the ambient lighting details are finalized—a globe-shaped candle placed in front of an aging Victorian crystal-framed mirror can illuminate a corner of the room that would have been a dark void otherwise.

While ambient lighting is mainly a matter of filling in the dark spaces with warm glows, the task becomes tricky in the nest when you consider that a room's lighting needs change drastically during the course of a day.

A room that features a wall of south-facing windows may offer more light than you need, creating a disturbing glare and contrast with the opposite side of the room that sits in the dark. To even out such a discrepancy, consider sheer curtains, shades, or adjustable blinds that are easy to manipulate during the day, limiting glare and allowing only the amount of light that you need into your nest. At the same time, consider placing a large mirror on the wall opposite this bank of windows. It will capture and reflect the light, brightening up that side of the room.

Dimmers on overhead lights or three way switches on lamps are another easy way to adjust the ambient light in a room, especially if you need to limit the sources of light in a room due to space or your budget. A three-way lamp will glow at its lowest wattage during a midnight confession of *amore* to your current lover, then provide a strong reading light at its height when you're home alone with *Vogue*. A dimmer for the dining-room chandelier allows you to crank down the wattage for romantic dinners, but gives the punch you need when using the same table for sewing curtains or mapping out your next backpacking trip.

Candles in front of mirrors or wall sconces on either side of a mirror have a similar way of doubling the light in a space. Even highly reflective metals, such as silver and polished brass can capture the light in a dark corner and magnify it, lightening up an otherwise darkened space.

Speaking of candles, these are one of the most accessible tools for ambient lighting. They flicker, creating dancing shadows across a table or wall. Many of them have delicious scents. And even those that just burn wax give off a faint whiff of romance, don't you think?) They come in all sizes, colors, and shapes, giving you a variety of options for focusing the height and wattage of light. And many are so artistic, you barely want to burn them, so they offer a room a decorative element to boot.

Votive candles lined along the ledge at the top of wainscoting double to draw the eye to that architectural feature while lighting up a dark side of the room. A cluster of mismatched white candles on a coffee table can lighten up an offering of hors d'oeuvres during cocktails. Placed in a brown bag half filled with sand, votive candles offer an amber glow along any entry pathway during holiday parties Santa Fe style.

Ambient lighting is particularly important when establishing a festive mood. A series of Christmas tree lights woven across a ceiling brightens up an entire room without any other decorations. Lining a window or following the lines of a fireplace mantle, twinkling string lights define an architectural feature as well as emit a soft glow where placed.

Tiki torches in the backyard, oil lamps from a camping store, a spotlight aimed toward the branches of an old oak tree, Christmas lights dangled en masse randomly from the top of an old fence—these bright, out-of-the-ordinary lights all offer a festive feel to an otherwise quiet, restive outdoor party space, creating the mood most parties crave for successful ambiance. When you can't afford top-of-the-line champagne for all your guests, I say spend a few extra bucks on some soft outdoor lighting—not too bright, or your guests might be able to read the label of what you're serving!

There's one more way to create ambient light in a room—place a light source outside of the room's windows. Doing so expands the space inside, because you can now see out of the window onto a deck

> "I made a pair of sconces from two scroll-shaped iron flower-pot holders—the iron scroll holds the light fixture and a pretty glass globe covers the bulb. I made another pair of lamps from two unusable clarinets purchased from an instrument repair shop, finishing the look with lampshades covered in decoupage sheets of music."
>
> —*Lana, twenty-nine, from Los Angeles*

or garden or tree branches instead of staring into a black mirror and your reflection. In small nests, a well-placed outdoor spotlight can do wonders for increasing the size of your space at night.

a blurb on bulbs

Most of us are familiar with the standard pear-shaped incandescent lightbulb that you buy at Safeway. These accommodate most household 120-volt currents and yield a warm light in various degrees of strength—40 watts, 60 watts, 100 watts.

You can purchase them in clear glass, which gives a bright white light, or in frosted or "pearl"-coated glass, which softens the glow. They also come in a variety of colors, which is fun for parties. They also are available in full-spectrum light, which comes very close to mimicking natural daylight, ideal for task lighting.

The incandescent bulb is best for general overhead lighting and also works well for reading lamps. Unless you're going for the starving-artist or heroin-addict look in your nest, these bulbs look best when covered by a shade made of any type of soft material, from rice paper to silk, or a ceramic, mica, glass, or even stylized plastic covering.

All light fixtures are required to list the maximum wattage recommended for that particular fixture or lamp. In most cases, you'll want to go no higher than a sixty-watt bulb, if only because a wattage higher than that may dominate all other light sources in the room. There's also a slight worry of creating a hot spot on the lampshade, wall, or ceiling near that bulb if it is left on for days on end, which could cause a fire.

It's worth mentioning that there are decorative bulbs that are meant to be shown off. I have several exposed bulbs shaped like candle flames in my nest. One is even tinted with amber glass, which accentuates its flame-like appearance. I use it for a wall sconce that's shaped like an old-fashioned candlestick holder. I've seen flame-shaped bulbs that are even manufactured to flicker like a candle (which may or may not appeal to your senses). To each her own.

Globe bulbs, like the kind you see in Hollywood dressing rooms, are also meant to be shown off rather than hidden by a shade or glass covering. And silver-capped bulbs, which look as though they have been dipped in melted pewter on the fat end, offer a nice even light about the room without glare, especially if used with a pendant or track fixtures that project light downward. When you gaze up at these bulbs, you only see the silver tip and a nice glow surrounding it.

While fluorescent lights don't usually make the top ten of most nesters' wish lists, it is worth noting that fluorescent bulbs and tubes do come in a wide range of hues, yielding warm and cool colors of light. They last longer than incandescent bulbs, which is a plus, and they do produce fantastic shadow-free light for tasks such as doing laundry or cleaning out the cat box.

Halogen bulbs make spectacular spotlights, because they produce a strong white light perfect for showing off artwork or sculpture. They also make fantastic reading lights in work areas because the light is so bright. The only drawback is that halogen bulbs become very hot when left on for long periods of time, so make sure that you don't leave yours on for hours on end.

when a fixture is a feature

Light fixtures are decorative features for any living space. Choose one that complements the era of your home—a groovy plastic bee's nest of a chandelier in a 1960s pad, a mock gas lamp in a turn-of-the-century bungalow. And they add a splash of texture, color, and visual interest to any part of your nest that needs that extra something.

When choosing a light fixture for your nest, the stakes are not as high as, say, picking a wall color or textiles for curtains. Most light stores will let you take the fixture home for twenty-four hours and try it out in the room, which is the best way to assess how it looks in the space, and more important, see how it casts light around the room. After all, that should be the deciding factor in your purchase. If the pendant lamp you love projects light onto your dining-room table as though you are about to perform a surgery, well, that ain't appetizing.

The main question in choosing a fixture, then, is to determine how much light the overhead fixture or wall sconce needs to project into the space and whether it should be directed light for a specific task, like cooking or reading, or simply assist in the room's ambiance. How to go about deciding that?

NESTING PLEASURES:
REPLACE THAT UGLY
DIME-STORE FIXTURE

Materials:
One captivating ceiling or wall sconce fixture
Ladder (and a second pair of hands to help you steady it)
Screwdriver
Wire strippers
Lineman pliers
Wire nuts

1. Turn off the electrical circuit to that particular fixture at your main power box. If you're not sure which switch operates the room you are in, turn the entire power off in the house or apartment and work during the day when there's plenty of natural light.

2. Remove the old fixture by unscrewing the metal or plastic cover plate that attaches the fixture to the metal fixture box hidden inside the ceiling or wall. If you see a mounting bar, which is about the size of a small metal Popsicle stick, unscrew that, too. Look for two wires or groups of wires—one black, one white.

3. Have a friend hold the old fixture while you free it from these black and white wires. You will need to remove the electrical tape or unscrew the wire nuts that keep the two connected, and then untwist the wires. If you failed to turn off the power, you will probably realize so at this point. Don't say I didn't warn you! Electrical shock is a serious concern, so take

all safety precautions seriously. And if you are at all insecure about doing this on your own, please hire an electrician or handyman (or woman) to do the deed.

4. Once free, place the old dusty fixture in the trash or recycling bin.

5. On your new sensual light fixture, use wire strippers to strip about one-half inch of the insulation covering its own set of black and white wires. Once exposed, have your friend hold the fixture while you connect the wires to those in the ceiling or wall—white goes with white, black goes with black.

6. To connect these wires, hold the two white wires and twist them together in a clockwise direction using the lineman pliers. Then, place them in a wire nut and twist the nut in a clockwise direction.

7. Repeat with both sets of black wires.

8. If your new fixture has one exposed copper wire (likely), you must look to see if the fixture box has one, too. (Look for either a bare copper wire or one encased in green insulation.) This is called a ground wire and, without getting too technical, is a safety precaution built into most new homes' electrical systems. Older homes don't have them, in which case, you may just ignore this wire coming out of your new fixture. Otherwise, bond the two wires together with a wire nut, the same as you did with the black and white wires.

9. Wires connected, shove them all back into the wall or ceiling, being careful not to loosen the connections, and attach the new canopy or cover, taking care that the new fixture sits straight and level on the wall or ceiling. You're done!

The overall light emitted by a fixture is determined by two factors—the wattage of bulb you use and the amount of light that penetrates through the mica, ceramic, paper, silk, or plastic shade that conceals the bulb.

If you desire more light than your wattage allows—remember, maximum wattage should be indicated on the fixture—consider the shape and color of the shade used to conceal the bulb.

Lighter shades in neutral colors allow the light to seep through them, which then projects more light into the room. Darker shades prevent light from seeping out from the shade except where the shade is open. The tops and bottoms of bell-shaped shades in darker colors, then, yield stronger, more directed light, which may be ideal for, say, a reading lamp by the bed, since the light will fall strongly across the pages of your book, and won't produce a glare in your or your sleeping lover's eyes.

The shape of the shade also determines the amount of light emitted into a room. Shades with broad bottoms will spread a wide diameter of light below them, leaving only a small glow coming from their tops. Cylinder-shaped shades emit an even distribution of light from above and below, yielding great ambiance, but very little direct light.

If what you're after is an accent light to heighten a ceiling or graze a wall, an uplight fixture is best for that particular purpose. Like a flaming torch, the tops of these shades flare out wider than the bottoms, yielding a cathedral glow aimed toward the heavens.

Accessories

Magpies are notorious for stealing shiny objects—wire, bottle tabs, aluminum foil—to decorate their twiggy nests.

 Like a pair of pearl earrings on an otherwise unadorned face, like a Kate Spade clutch paired with faded jeans, like a pair of Jimmy Choos (a girl can dream) with an inconspicuous black dress, accessories in the nest make or break the sensuality of your home in the same way an accessory can make or break an outfit. This is true, especially, if your nest is otherwise composed of nondescript belongings—a simple collection of Contemporary furnishings bathed in neutrals and barely-there textures.

Art, framed photos, trinkets collected while traveling, a book collection, plants, cabinetry hardware and other metal offerings, even a pet—these are the nesting accessories that add personality and sensual interest to your nest. These are what distinguish your nest from those photographed in the Pottery Barn catalogue, beautiful and restful as they may appear. These are what, ultimately, turn any old living space into a "home."

Like all aspects of nesting, there is a sensual way to accessorize your nest and a not-so-sensual approach. Too many tchotchkes crammed into a space can turn a potentially interesting and stimulating collection into a junky mishmash no one dares to ask about. Too many works of art hung haphazardly on a wall can turn that surface into a confusing distraction, not a stimulating visual feast.

When it comes to accessorizing your nest, less is often more. Let's discuss the most common accessories and how to maximize their sensuality.

art and photographs

First, let's get one thing straight: All art is visually sensual, no matter what your taste or preferences—be it abstract prints, oil paintings, or delicate watercolors. So this section isn't going to tell you what type of art to acquire for your nest. It will only direct you on the display of your acquisitions.

Hence, we'll cover just two key issues here: (1) How to frame your artwork and beloved photographs, and (2) how to arrange them on the walls.

Choosing a Frame

Whether your art is signed and original, a mass-produced print like the kind you buy at MoMA, or a series of family portraits, you will want to frame it to avoid the college-dorm look in your nest. Frames are important tools for keeping the eye focused on the art, containing its image and separating it from its surroundings. If your walls have elaborate patterns or textures on them, a frame will distinguish the art from its busy background. The goal is to complement the image. Here's how:

Pick a style. Frames, like furniture, come in a variety of styles. There's the traditional or classical frame—an elaborately carved wooden frame, often gilded, like the kind you see associated with rich, heavy oil paintings. And then there's the simple wooden frame lightly stained or left in its natural state, such as you often see with pencil or ink drawings, charcoal sketches, and watercolors. For more modern pieces of art, metal or painted wooden frames complement the boldness or abstract quality of that style. When choosing the style, you want the frame to not only complement the style of art, but also the style of your furnishings so it won't stand out in the room like a sore thumb.

Choose a color. Similarly, you want the color of your frame to complement the art. If the art has bold, rich colors, you'll want a frame with rich, solid tones—a mahogany stain, Chinese lacquered red, shiny copper—to match the intensity of the art. For art with muted tones, say a series of pastel drawings or a seascape watercolor, you'll want a sedated frame to match the delicacy of the art—an unstained maple, a simple gold-painted frame, or a pine frame colorwashed in a pale green tone.

Sometimes an effective approach is to choose one color from the work and match it to the color of the frame. A painting of a robin's nest, primarily in tones of brown except for the eggs, might only come to life when framed in pale blue.

Match the weight of the frame to the heftiness of the art. Likewise, the size of the frame should complement the weight of the art. A wide, concave-shaped frame that reaches out toward the eye best serves heavier images—say, an oil painting of a train snaking up a smoky mountain—whereas a narrow, simple silver or black frame complements the lightness of, say, a lithograph drawing or an ink sketch. A bold graphic poster deserves a stately silver or black frame (not the clip-art variety) to set it off without distracting from the designs. Mounting this type of art directly onto a piece of wood or steel is another stunning approach to consider.

Choose an appropriate mat, when needed. Not every piece of art needs a mat board, which is a cardboard cutout separating the work of art from the glass, serving as a visual transition between the art and frame. Typically, you'll want to use a mat with watercolors, drawings, pastels, and photos. Mat boards not only provide some visual distance between the image and frame, but also help protect the art from condensation by adding a very thin layer between the art and the glass. The mat should be acid free to further protect the art.

When using a mat, there are several design considerations—how wide to go between the image and frame, what color or texture to use, and whether you'd like any other details such as decorative wash lines or designs or the use of double mats to further set off the image. When in doubt, an ivory or off-white mat is typically safe. However, a lightly colored mat using a tone picked up from the art itself can have a bold effect. Darker toned mats may overwhelm the image, though not always—it's really an intuitive decision and one that takes some experimenting with the art you have.

Size may vary from three-quarters of an inch to several inches wide. Typically, wider mats will draw the eye into the image, giving it more substance—this is often effective with small works of art that might otherwise get lost on a large wall. A bold work, on the other hand needs only a small bordering mat—if any at all—to give it adequate space, or visual distance, from its frame.

The Art of Display

There is truly an art to displaying art, which is why museums have curators and committees for their collection displays. With the following key principles in mind, your nest will not only embrace your artwork in the most sensual manner possible but also show it off not unlike a gallery might.

- **Match the art to the wall space.** If you have a tall, skinny wall, consider a Chinese scroll to fit the space, a long, thin poster, or a series of artwork or photos that adhere to one theme—family portraits, landscapes, sketches of flowers. The latter option, gallery style, is most effective if the art is all the same size and/or is mounted in similar frames, spaced the same distance apart. A horizontal space, say, the area above the mantel or sofa, is best enhanced with art displayed horizontally—span the series mentioned above along the length of the mantel or wall or choose a piece of art that is more wide than tall.

- **Group a series of art together rather than spreading the pieces about the nest.** The overall effect—say, an image of one tree photographed or drawn during each season—is far more visually potent when viewed en masse than when dispersed about the room.

- **Display a series in a corner.** A collection of watercolors of the Miami coast painted in the 1920s by my great-great-grandmother hang on the two walls of one corner in my dining room. Because of their placement, they seem to be addressing each other. Guests *always* ask about them (but when I used to hang them on one wall side by side, they rarely got comment). We've placed a dracaena potted tree (which looks like a miniature palm) in front of these paintings, and the combination of real palm and painted palm is truly stunning, so our visitors say.

• **Keep the lower edge of your frames consistent.** This gives a sturdy base to your artwork. The tops of your frames may form peaks and valleys along the wall, since they are not likely to be all the same height, but the bottom edge will be as solid as rock, creating a calm, sturdy visual.

• **Whether they are photos, paintings, or a mixture of both, aim to echo the shape of the space.** Whether the space is a rectangle, a square, a triangle (which might match the wall space of a stairwell), keep the edges of the images straight as you first create the overall shape of the grouping. Then fill in the center with whatever frames fit, all of which may be different sizes and shapes.

• **When grouping photographs on a tabletop, vary the scale and subject matter.** So advises Joyal Watkins, an interior designer in Chicago. "I mix people, places, and animals in various sizes," he says. "You don't want ten eight-by-tens clumped together on a table. The eye will tell you if the grouping is interesting or not."

• **Consider the purpose of the art.** Laura, thirty-two, from Warren, Michigan, uses a huge reprint of *A Streetcar Named Desire* by Thomas Hart Benton as a focal point in her living room. Lana, twenty-nine, from Los Angeles, uses art for distraction—she hung a two-by-three-foot poster of a work by Bouguereau (think lush) over the toilet so it's the first thing she sees—not the WC—when she walks in. Art may also serve as an excellent conversation starter, especially if it reveals something about you. Jeanette, twenty-eight, from Castro Valley, California, displays a print of her favorite opera, while Drew, thirty-three, from Danbury, Connecticut, devotes an entire wall in her dining room to old family portraits, all in black and white. She even turns colored photos into black and white, to fit the theme.

• **Don't limit your artwork to the public areas of your nest.** Kate, twenty-nine, from Grand Rapids, Michigan, has hung a friend's work of art on the wall opposite the foot of her bed. "It completely changes the space, giving the bedroom more intention and design," she says. Alice, thirty-four, from San Diego, also loves the art in her bedroom. She limits the genre, though, to abstract art and Japanese calligraphy. "This was a conscious decision," she says. "We didn't want to be reminded of anything that might stress us out. Our aim was to make the bedroom a neutral place, disconnected from the everyday world."

MY ART, MYSELF

"I framed my great-grandfather's drafting school artwork: 'Details of Door Panels,' from 1898, along with some sketches from the fifties dug out of a Chicago museum's trash."   —*Zoe, thirty-three, from Dallas*

"We framed photographs of all the places my husband and I have lived."   —*Reese, twenty-nine, from Cleveland, Ohio*

"My husband and I love trying new restaurants. We framed menus from some of our favorites and hung them in our dining room."   —*Katie, twenty-six, from Chicago*

"We have some nice art pieces from our travels to Indonesia that are unique and interesting. I love that they are not something anyone can buy from Pottery Barn."

—*Blanca, twenty-eight, from Exeter, New Hampshire*

"I have a few simple frames I use to display a rotating collection of Indian movie star postcards."

—*Magda, twenty-four, from Tiffin, Ohio*

"My husband and I have a friendship room with pictures of us and our friends. That way, our guests can see for themselves that they are still a part of our lives."

—*Maria, thirty, from Brooklyn, New York*

"We have lots of small snapshots grouped on end tables. I like to put a plant or potpourri and a candle next to each, kind of like little altars."

—*Laura, thirty-two, from Warren, Michigan*

"Our fridge is completely covered with photos. These are great for when a guest is standing by, unattended, while you're doing food prep for a party: 'What was Jamaica like?'"

—*Olive, twenty-eight, from Boston*

"I collect original artwork from places we've traveled—a painting of a monkey from Costa Rica, a portrait of a man's head from Prague."

—*Alice, thirty-four, from San Diego*

collections displays

Why display your knickknacks, your obsessions, your trinkets around the nest? Chicago interior designer Joyal Watkins explains: "Collections personalize a home and add layers of interest to a room." They also add a sense of permanence or richness to a home, because, typically, it takes a long time to fully develop a collection.

Collections reveal so much about a nester. Their passions, for instance. Veronica, twenty-eight, from Los Angeles, has a lot of coffee paraphernalia in her kitchen—she loves coffee. And Gretchen, thirty-two, from St. Paul, Minnesota, displays a purse collection on the wall of her home office/guest room. She calls it her "wall-o-purses." "I love little black purses and think it's a shame to just store them in a drawer. So, I hang them on the wall. Right now I have about six, all black, all evening bags."

In addition to one's obsessions, a collection may also serve to reveal a sense of humor. Zoe, thirty-three, from Dallas, has a collection of talking clocks around her home. What started as a joke collection from her father is now a real collection of about ten, she says. Lana, twenty-nine, from Los Angeles, collects pug figurines, mostly purchased while traveling. She has little pug statues from Paris, Florence, Budapest, Vienna, and St. Petersburg, among other places, and displays them on two shelves. Her real pug, Olivia, brings the inanimate to life.

The key to making a statement with your collections, rather than presenting what might, to the careless eye, look like a bunch of junk (no offense) crammed onto a shelf, is to arrange your objects purposefully.

"Every collection display needs a focal point," says Watkins. "The focal point can be the largest item or the most colorful." The focal point is the most important piece in the collection, and it is around this that the other pieces are arranged. Without a focal point, says Watkins, nothing in the collection is noticeable. A collection needs variance in color and shape to really make a statement, he says.

What to avoid? Putting things too close together, warns Watkins. "Depending on the scale of your objects, each one needs breathing space. But they also need to be close enough to relate. It's an intuitive decision."

🐦 *Go-Girl Guidance* 🐦

Don't forget to accessorize the bathroom—your daily evening escape, not to mention a five-minute escape for visitors, too. Blanca, twenty-eight, from Exeter, New Hampshire, tapes pretty cards to the back of her bathroom door "so people have something to look at while they sit instead of feeling claustrophobic."

Zoe, thirty-three, from Dallas, accessorizes her bathroom with a blue transparent plastic toilet seat, which always gets comments. "It was cheap and gives the bathroom so much personality," she says. Lana, twenty-nine, from Los Angeles, fashioned a bunch of coral-colored fabric roses into a garland, which she wound around her bathroom mirror. And because her bathroom had no windows to the outside world, Molly, thirty-two, from San Francisco, placed several framed photos of "outside stuff" in the room.

flora . . .

Plants: They are alive, rich with texture and color and sometimes patterns, scented in some cases, flowering in others. And, they are good for the home environment, since they absorb airborne pollutants, such as cleaning products and home-office equipment pollutants. What's more, they provide oxygen and humidity to the air.

Not only are plants an inexpensive accessory, but they are also easily replaced if they don't work within the space we had in mind for them when we saw them. Or, if we accidentally neglect them and they die. But the real beauty of plants as accessories for the nest is that they can do so many different things. A glorious potted palm placed in front of a sun-flooded bay window, (a window which unfortunately overlooks a toxic wasteland across the street) becomes that room's focal point. Your new indoor view not only distracts from the disaster across the street that makes those bay windows your nest's greatest disappointment, but also provides a natural curtain, diffusing the light from the sun into your living room and blocking the view just enough to give you the semi-privacy you may desire in that part of your nest.

If your thumb is more flesh toned than green, starting an indoor garden might be too much of a challenge for you. Begin by picking out one or two hardy and inexpensive plants that are known for their survival skills even during long periods of neglect. Any plant store-owner can point you to those specimens, but before you hit the store, you must take note of the conditions in your nest or the parts of your nest where you wish to grow plants. A plant specialist can't do a thing for you if he or she doesn't know how much sunlight your apartment gets.

The most critical conditions to note are sunlight, warmth, and humidity. All plants thrive in different combinations of these, so for a successful indoor garden, you'll want to pick the types of flora that will have the most success in your particular microclimate. A southwest-facing sunny window that receives direct sunlight for more than five hours a day is a warm, bright spot that probably has a lower amount of moisture in the air than, say, a bathroom or kitchen window that faces east. A cactus might thrive in that sunny window, while a fern would do lovely in the high humidity and low light of the loo.

Go-Girl Guidance

Wish your radiator had a more sensual purpose than hissing throughout the midnight hours? Use it as a pedestal for plants. Have a hardware store cut a half-inch-thick piece of fireproof insulating board to lay over the top of your radiator. Upon this, place a wooden tray filled with a plastic or glass tray lined with pebbles. Use that as a shelf upon which you may place several containers of leafy plants. The insulation will keep the plants safe from the heat and the pebbles will collect run-off water after feedings. Keeping water in the pebbles will also raise the humidity level around the plants as it slowly evaporates from the radiator heat.

In addition to the approximate hours of direct sunlight, it's also important to consider how the sunlight changes during certain times of year. In winter, when the sun hangs low in the sky, you may see more direct light than during the summer, when the sun is overhead and shaded by the eaves of your roof. This shouldn't have an effect on what type of plant you purchase as long as you realize you might need to move it to a sunnier spot in the summer.

Equally important is to note the average temperature of your nest. If you never turn on the heat and you live in Minnesota during the winter, you will need plants that thrive in frigid temperatures (as well as a therapist, perhaps, to discuss your self-destructive tendencies, but that's none of my business.) Similarly, if you live in the Arizona desert but keep your nest at a crisp sixty degrees, all those indoor cacti you collect might not look so hot after a while.

Once you've determined the conditions of your nest in the areas you'd like to display a plant or a grouping of plants, consider how you want those plants to occupy that space. Start with the plant's shape. Do you want the plant to serve as an architectural feature, a focal point in the room? If so, are you seeking height and interesting angles? Or would you prefer a broad canopy of leaves so the plant fills unused space and, perhaps, rounds out the corners of a room?

Next, consider the texture of the leaves. Do you want wispy, feathery leaves to soften harsh angles in a space? Or, are you looking for spikes to contrast your feather-soft nest? Finally, think about color and patterns. Leaves come in every shade of green, and many are more along the lines of gold or red or purple. Patterns are an option, too—some leaves are spotted, while others are striped. And many come in variegated patterns that give you two tones for one. Others have the added bonus of flowering on occasion, which is another consideration as you begin to accessorize with plants.

NESTING PLEASURES:
DESIGN AN INDOOR OASIS

Materials:

Three or more plants of various heights, colors, and textures

Plant stands or other display accessories

Pots or containers with saucers for water runoff

Rocks

Dirt

Handheld shovel

1. Pick the location for your indoor garden. Your options are limitless—a deep, sunny windowsill is the perfect locale for a varied herb garden in summer; plant a variety of fern species in an empty indirectly lit corner of the dining room; fill your sun-flooded entryway with potted palms and tropical exotics.

2. Plan the arrangement. In any grouping of plants, you'll want to establish a focal point—the tallest plant of the bunch. Group the other plants in relation to this focal point, which needn't be in the center of the group, but should be closest to the wall, with shorter plants in front and to the sides.

3. Choose your containers wisely. So they won't overwhelm the garden or the space in your nest, match the style of the pot or container with that of your furnishings. Simple ceramic or terra-cotta pots are best in country or contemporary settings, while metal or concrete containers blend in perfectly

in the modern-clad pad. Usually, plain colors—especially those in earth tones—serve the plant best, since they won't compete with nature.

4. If your container is purely decorative (it doesn't have a drainage hole in the bottom), fill it with a layer of pebbles or small rocks so the water can drain and not soak the roots of your plant. Then, fill the pot with dirt and transfer the plant, filling in with more dirt so the roots are snug in their new bed. If the container has a drainage hole, you may simply fill the pot with dirt and transfer the plant. Always place a saucer underneath these containers to catch the runoff when you water.

5. Think small. Before you know how proper a plant parent you are, start with just a few plants—one large, the other small and more replaceable, just in case that thumb of yours turns blue. Besides, a few sturdy, healthy plants often makes a grander statement than dozens of small unremarkable plants—especially if half of them are on their deathbeds.

. . . and fauna

Animal activists, please don't take me to court on this section. I don't mean to insult your pet by demoting him or her to a mere accessory in your nest. Heck, in San Francisco, it's not even kosher to call ourselves pet "owners." We are "pet guardians" out here, thank you very much.

Furthermore, I'm not at all suggesting we all get pets just to accessorize our nests. However, every animal lover I know wouldn't hesitate to agree that having a pet does increase the sensuality of the nest. And while Fluffy is not an essential aspect of our nest's structure, home just wouldn't be home without him or her. (Besides, where else can I cover the topic of pets in this book if not in the chapter about all those personal touches that make our nests our own?)

Truth is, pets are the ultimate sensual accessory in the nest, don't you think? They're soft, cuddly, furry, mobile (so you can take them with you in whatever room you choose to nest in at the moment). They are conversation starters. And they provide music to our ears when they bark, twerp, meow, or squeak in delight at seeing us when we come home at the end of the day. With a pet in the house, we never nest alone.

But, they can also be smelly (come on, let's be frank), loud when upset, and a slight nuisance when we want to leave town or even stay late at work or go out for a drink before coming home. Hence, a little pet advice is in order for those who are considering getting the ultimate accessory for their nest.

To maximize the sensual aspects of your pet, a nester must strive to de-emphasize the less-desirable aspects (the smell, the poo-poo accidents, the wear and tear on upholstery and rugs that comes with the territory). Here are two key things to assist you on that note.

Cleanliness Is Next to Dogliness

Grooming your pet is essential to keeping your nest sensual. That means regular brushing, bathing (for pets that need it—you know who you are), and cage or bed cleaning. Always scrub your pet's food dishes after each use or at least once a day if dry food is left out, just as you would clean your own dishes. This will not only help eliminate smells, but will also prevent bugs and rodents from taking interest in your nest. Besides, your pet deserves clean plates for his or her own health.

Cat litter boxes are best kept in discreet locations. If you have a back entryway or a separate laundry room that is large enough to accommodate a litter box, this would be ideal as opposed to keeping the litter in your own bathroom or your kitchen. If your nest simply lacks the space for a discreet location, perhaps attempt to distract from it by placing it behind a row of potted trees and plants, so the eye is drawn to greenery, not a plastic box. Oh, and by all means, use the smell-eliminating litter and a cover. Also, clean the box regularly. A pet-scented nest is hardly sensual.

In addition to keeping all the pet paraphernalia clean, you will need to clean your own nest more often because of the cat hair or dog slime or other pet debris that accumulates daily. Keeping the pet paraphernalia in a basket, drawer, or one designated spot in the nest will prevent that pet-junked look that your home might otherwise assume.

A Happy Pet Makes for Happy Nesting

Bonding with your pet is a critical part of nesting with him or her for two reasons: (1) Why have a pet if you don't enjoy the love? And (2) a neglected pet is an unhappy animal, which makes your time in the nest spent with him or her a constant battle. What's more, an unhappy pet will turn to destructive behavior and wreak havoc in your home, tearing the upholstery to shreds, peeing (or worse) on your beloved rugs, clawing at the refinished wood in your formal dining room.

If you find yourself scolding your pet more than loving him or her, it might be time to evaluate your behavior and consider a little

pet therapy or training. This will not only will teach Cleo how to behave in a humanly-acceptable manner, but will also teach *you* how to
be a better "guardian." As for your nest? It will once again become
your home tweet home.

FLOWER ARRANGEMENTS

Whether you're grouping fresh cuttings from
your garden or making a bouquet with a few flower-shop favorites, keep the following tips in mind:

• **For an informal, or romantic look, combine flowers
in pale tones, round blossoms, and feathery foliage in a
loose arrangement.** Hold them in everyday objects found
about the kitchen—a wide-brimmed ceramic pitcher, a wine
decanter, a simple glass.

• **For a more sculptural or modern look, stick with
one or two bold colors, architectural or spiky foliage,
and blossoms with interesting geometric shapes—lilies,
birds-of-paradise, gladiolas.** Place your bouquet in glass
containers or vases in bold colors that contrast the main hue of
the bouquet. Metal or sculptured vases also accommodate
modern arrangements quite nicely.

• **Always establish a focal point in the bouquet.** To
create this, start the arrangement with your tallest flowers or
decorative branch, then arrange the fuller flowers—roses,
tulips, lilies, irises—around this mast. These blossoms are
what becomes the focal point of your bouquet—they are what
the eye typically takes in first and they establish the overall

effect. Finish the bouquet with greenery or smaller blossoms in complementary colors for a harmonious arrangement or use contrasting hues for an electric effect.

• **Pick a shape for your bouquet.** The most common shapes include the Fan (the blossoms form an arch that resembles an open hand fan), the Vertical (think of a dozen calla lilies in a skinny vase), the Horizontal (flowers spill outward rather than upward, often effected in bowl-shaped vases), the Inverted T (imagine a spike of flowers in the center, with blossoms and greenery reaching outward, horizontally, at the bottom), and the Triangle (shaped exactly like one), the Circle (flowers form a perfect sphere, with blossoms shooting upward, to the sides, and angled downward, below the rim of the vase).

• **The shape of your arrangement should complement the area where your bouquet stands.** The Inverted T is often great for mantels because the tall center provides an excellent vertical focus, but the sides fill out the mantel surface. The horizontal arrangement, on the other hand, is perfect for dining-room tables, since it won't block views when guests are seated across from each other. A vertical arrangement of gladiolas looks stunning on a square receiving table in a narrow hallway.

• **For proper proportions, a bouquet should stand approximately one and a half times the height and width of its container.** It should also be in scale with the area in which it is placed. In other words, avoid the mass-sized three-foot-tall arrangement on your teeny-tiny coffee table. Floating gardenias in small glass bowls would be a better coffee table match, saving the gargantuan bouquet for your rich uncle's marble foyer.

- **When in doubt about your arrangement, just remember: Less is always more.** White tulips in simple glass vases are the epitome of classic elegance.

Welcoming the Flock

Male bowerbirds weave dramatic arches out of sticks and twigs, decorating them with bright blue flowers, berries, even inanimate objects, to lure and impress potential mates.

 Nesting alone has its perks—everything is in its place. Or, if it's out of place, we know where to hunt it down. And no one is telling us how to live our lives, paint our walls, or clean up the kitchen.

The real beauty of nesting alone, though, is that we can invite our friends, family, and loved ones over whenever we want, sharing our sensual nest with them in our own unique way and on our own terms (except for the surprise guest now and then who makes rude suggestions on how to improve our lifestyle).

Opening our home to others is sharing a part of ourselves with them—our sensibilities, our peace of mind, our space, our retreat from the maddening world, our shelter, our safety, and our food. Welcoming the flock is one of the most intimate acts among humans and animals alike.

True nesters believe it is one of the most rewarding, too. Drinking a bottle of wine in the comfort of home is far more an intimate exchange than screaming over loud music in a smoky bar (not to suggest there isn't a time and place for that, too, let's be clear). Being inside one's home is a quieter, more revealing exchange because so much of the nester's personality is apparent in her own surroundings. It's sort of a psychic revelation, hanging out in someone's home. Details about the way their furniture is arranged, the colors they choose to decorate, and their prized possessions on display can reveal so much about their beliefs and dreams and values.

However, welcoming the flock is not always instinctive behavior. In fact, it is a learned act, formed partly from our childhood experiences of family gatherings and hosting birthday parties and sleepovers, and partly by observing the successful hosting of others. While not everyone is a natural host, sensual welcoming can be learned, even if you didn't live in an open-door nest growing up. Unfortunately, I can't cover every nuance of welcoming the flock into your nest in this little chapter at the end of the book, but here are at least a few basics.

the drop-in guest

Not everyone shares this view, but I happen to love it when friends drop by for a visit. The arrival is unexpected and (usually) very well appreciated. There is something familial and comforting about a friend who stops by on a whim to see if you're home to just hang out. Especially on foggy or rainy days when you have nothing going on anyway.

But for those whose lifestyles are so scheduled that any rare moment spent at home is so savagely coveted, a visit feels more obligatory or inconvenient than fun or delightfully unexpected. I respect that. But I'd also suggest reexamining your lifestyle. Perhaps you could use a little more downtime, eh?

The accidental host never wants to feel unprepared, because that might lead to stress, which is surely the opposite of what your guest had intended by his or her visit. To avoid this, it helps to stock your nest with a few drop-in guest treats and back-pocket ideas for welcoming them into your home, no matter how brief their stay.

Let's start with that welcoming part. Since it's often scary and intimidating for a guest to drop by, given that many of us are so busy these days that private life is often considered a sacred Do Not Disturb, it helps to be clear right off the bat on whether or not the visit is, in fact, desirable.

Before you answer that door, then, decide if you want the interaction and, if so, how long the ideal visit may be. Once that's clear in your mind, you know how to proceed with your guest:

- "Hey, that's so great you stopped by! I was just about to do five weeks' worth of laundry because I'm traveling on business tomorrow. Want to help me fold my underwear over a bottle of wine?" (If your guest does, indeed, stay and help, he or she deserves more than wine—be sure to break out your chocolate reserves, too.)
- "Hi! I was just trying to figure out what to do with myself today. Come in and sit! What would you like to drink?"
- "Thanks so much for stopping by. I was just about to take a nap, though—I think I may be coming down with a stomach virus and would hate to make you sick. Are you around Tuesday night instead?"

However you respond, it's often comforting for the visitor to know they are not intruding, which is relatively easy to indicate by your welcoming line. You can always, for instance, throw in a: "I love it when friends stop by!" Also, if you welcome the visit, but want to keep it short, it helps a guest to know that right off the bat so there's no ambiguity. So, you can dance around in delight when they knock on your door, but be clear about the fact that you only have an hour before you have to buckle down and clean the house because you promised yourself you'd do it that day.

Aside from your welcoming line, it's useful to have a few ideas in the back of your head for shaping the visit, so your drop-bys don't feel awkwardly intrusive. If you are right in the middle of doing something, like squeezing oranges, put your guest to work after you greet him or her with a hug and offer of food or drink (more on this in a minute). The reward is fresh juice after the hard work is done.

Sometimes sharing a task works as a nice icebreaker, especially for the guest you don't know very well, because he or she feels suddenly useful and appreciated. A very close friend or family member will likely jump in to help with what you're doing, so you needn't worry about awkward moments or making the person feel like they are at home. I mentioned folding laundry before, but weeding the garden, organizing photos for albums, even doing crafty things, like potting some bulbs you have lying around may all be appropriate if this is what you were in the middle of doing when your guest came a-knocking.

Otherwise, the usual entertaining tricks may all be applied to a surprise guest: conversation (if you're at a loss, ask your guest about himself or herself—who doesn't like to talk about themselves?), music, an old video you've both wanted to see that you happen to have in your collection, even baking if you want to get nostalgic about those box-brownie days that were the start of many friendships in middle school. Which brings us around to food.

Offering a surprise guest something to eat and drink is standard protocol. In the morning: coffee, tea, hot cocoa, a Bloody Mary, even champagne are all appropriate beverages. (Note: If you develop a reputation for serving champagne to your guests, you'll probably never have to worry about being alone on a Sunday morning!) Mid-day and afternoon beverages may range from tea and coffee to soda, bubbly water, and any variety of alcoholic beverages you may keep on hand.

🐦 Go-Girl Guidance 🐦

How to avoid eating up your guest treats between those surprise visits? Three ways:

- **Hide it.** For her guests, Drew, thirty-three, from New Hartford, New York, keeps a hidden bottle of champagne in the salad drawer of her refrigerator so she doesn't have to see it everyday (and be tempted to open it). Madison, twenty-eight, from Westfield, New Jersey, keeps her guest food in a hard-to-reach cabinet that requires her to bend down to get it—so she usually doesn't.
- **Freeze it.** Kate, twenty-nine, from Grand Rapids, Michigan, keeps a batch of homemade cookie dough in the freezer—a delightful treat for guests that requires too much effort for everyday snacking. Justine, thirty-one, from Mountain View, California, keeps an oversized box of frozen profiteroles from

Costco. "The only reason I don't indulge on my own is because they live in the freezer and I don't normally look there for snacks. Plus, you have to wait thirty minutes for them to thaw."

• **Stock your least favorites.** That way, you're less likely to devour the supplies. Lana, twenty-nine, from Los Angeles, stocks her nest with stuff she is either allergic to or doesn't like—Coke, beer, potato chips, and scotch. For Kasey, twenty-five, from Hoboken, New Jersey, her standard guest snack is olives: "For me, olives would be in my fridge for all eternity!"

Snacks are always appreciated when offered, and the more surprising or out-of-the-ordinary the snack, the more delightful to your guest. Having exotic treats that you pull out only when company comes not only reveals that you are truly excited they stopped by and are willing to break out the good stuff for them, but also is such a nice, sensual break in everyday living for both you and your guest.

THE THINGS WE SERVE

"I keep strawberry daiquiri mix in the freezer, Captain Morgan or Bacardi to go with it, and ice cream for simple desserts."

—*Jasmine, twenty-nine, from Long Island, New York*

"Mango juice and rum, so I can whip up mango spritzers."

—*Jeanette, twenty-eight, from Castro Valley, California*

"We keep crackers, canned pâtés from France, cornichons, olives, artichoke paste, olive tapenade, and wine or sparkling wine for guests. Since we always have vegetables and yogurt in the house, we can always throw a dip together."

—*Leah, thirty-six, from Wichita, Kansas*

"Really good quality tea, regular and decaf coffee, and a few kinds of sodas or juice."

—*Meryl, twenty-nine, from Oakland, California*

"I keep cans of chickpeas to make hummus or to toast with spices for a cocktail-nut thing."

—*Carissa, thirty-five, from Chicago*

"We buy Pellegrino by the case and keep a few bottles in storage for guests. I also try to have that crunchy oriental mix stuff on hand. And, I always keep bacon, peas, and pine nuts in the freezer in case I have to pull together an interesting pasta dish with nothing in the fridge."

—*Sarah, thirty-six, from Kailua, Hawaii*

"I always have a salami drying in my fridge—people love it."

—*Claire, thirty-five, from Bellingham, Washington*

overnight guests

Sleepovers are never fun if your space is too tiny to allow a little breathing room between you and your guest. I had a friend in college who once asked to stay with me and my roommates after a trip abroad. After a few days of sharing my small futon in a room that could hold nothing more than the mattress, I asked her to move into the living area and sleep on the floor with pillows from the couch.

Well, my roommates soon grew tired of her stuff—everywhere!—so I had to ask her if she could stay with someone else. I didn't really think it was that big of a deal, but rumor has it that she was so disgusted by my lack of hospitality we haven't really spoken since.

The moral of the story (besides make a point to only befriend reasonable people): If your accommodations can't support a guest due to lack of space or roommates, then your only recourse is to keep a list of cheap hotels and B and Bs in your neighborhood and offer to make a reservation for your guests. Or, if you're really feeling gracious, sleep at your lover's palace while your friend crashes at yours.

Those with the luxury of a spare bedroom are better equipped to host overnight guests, but you don't necessarily need an extra room to pamper a friend for days and nights on end. All you need is some way to give both you and your guest a sense of privacy so that either of you can escape for downtime when the need arises.

Jennifer, thirty-two, from Concord, Georgia, shares her nest with several roommates, so when a guest comes to stay, he or she gets the fold-out sofa and the roommates close off the living room with a built-in hidden sliding door to make it private. "It works pretty well if everyone remembers to use the back door instead of the front, barging in on the unsuspecting guest at three a.m.," she says.

Screens work, too, especially if the space is as open as in a studio.

This is how Maria, thirty, from Brooklyn, New York, ensures her guests have privacy. "We always offer our guests our bedroom, but they usually say no. So, we invested in an air cushion and set it up behind a screen in the living room to give our guests some privacy or at least the illusion of privacy," she says.

Aside from privacy (or the illusion thereof), you'll naturally want to offer your guests the basics: clean sheets, blankets, towels, pillows, a quick tour of the house, including the bathroom and a rundown on how to work the shower, a walk through the kitchen with tips on where you keep the good stuff, and an open invitation for them to help themselves to anything they want or need around the house.

Molly, thirty-two, from San Francisco, goes as far as telling her guests that she'll make them stay at a hotel if they ask her, "Is it okay if I . . . ?" "They have to help themselves to any- and everything," she says. The goal is to make your guests feel like your home is their home, and offering the basics will just about do it.

Now, if you're the overachiever type and enjoy going the extra yard to make your guests feel as though they are on vacation, consider the following amenities. But beware: You may become a revolving hotel due to your graciousness!

- **Welcoming message.** Daisy, thirty-one, from Queens, New York, has a chalkboard in her dining area. She always writes a welcoming message when guests visit. It makes them feel so special, she says.
- **Fresh flowers.** Who doesn't love a vase of fresh flowers by the bed or makeshift bed, as the case may be? Especially if they are scented—roses, jasmine, gardenias, lilies, paper whites.
- **Water.** Another special touch is a glass or bottle of water by the bed. It can be quite intimidating, as a guest, to try to locate

a glass in the kitchen cupboards in the middle of the night when the throat is parched from the previous day's travel or the night's revelries.

• **Toiletries.** So your guest may experience a mini spa vacation while he or she stays, keep a collection of shampoos, lotions, soaps, and spare toothbrushes for overnight guests. Kristen, twenty-seven, from Greenville, South Carolina, has a basket under the sink with spare toiletries salvaged from mailbox samples, giving her guests a variety of products from which to choose in the event they forgot their own.

• **Top-of-the-line linens.** I mentioned towels and sheets as a basic offering for your guests, but if you really want to show off your nesting instincts, only offer the fluffiest, softest linens you own—not the old stuff you inherited from previous roommates. A soft feather comforter, flannel sheets, fluffy towels, and possibly a spare bathrobe—these are the details that turn a visit into an escape for your guests.

🐦 *Go-Girl Guidance* 🐦

"I always give my guests two towels each day they visit," says Maria, thirty, from Brooklyn, New York. "I don't want people to feel that they have to use the same towel after a shower. And women need two towels—one for their hair and one for their body."

• **Comfort food.** Preparing a meal for an overnight guest may be too much to handle, but if you're skilled in the kitchen, there's nothing like a home-cooked meal to welcome a friend. Jeanette, twenty-eight, from Castro Valley, California, always stocks the house with oranges when guests come to stay, "so I can make them fresh squeezed OJ in the morning," she says. Jennifer, thirty-two, from Concord, Georgia, is sure to have eggs on hand when she's expecting overnighters. "Frittatas and omelets are great and can easily incorporate garden vegetables or leftovers that might also be on hand," she says.

- **A mission.** Believe it or not, some guests will enjoy helping out with your daily errands. "It helps them feel like they are part of the family," says Olivia, thirty-one, from Berkeley, California, who often asks her visitors to run an easy errand if it is on their way.

- **Tourist tips.** If your guests are seeing your town for the first time, jot down a few must-sees and -dos for them to oc-cupy themselves with while you are at work or preoccupied with other commitments. Olivia, for instance, hands her guests a spare key and a short list of things they might enjoy doing, tailored to their particular interests, within walking distance of her nest. She always includes her work number so they can call if they have any questions.

- **Your signature touch.** Jessica, thirty-six, from Rome, likes to put a picture of her guests in a frame by their bed. "The sillier the picture, the better," she says. Leida, twenty-seven, from Seattle, always puts out lots of books, pictures, and magazines for her guests in case they have trouble sleep-ing or need to entertain themselves on their own for a while. Olive, twenty-eight, from Boston, who currently lives in San Francisco, keeps a stack of books specifically about San Fran-cisco to give her out-of-towners some local flavor. When pos-sible, place a small lamp on the bedside table for night reading. Tray tables are great for this—especially for guests sleeping on makeshift beds. And finally, a small travel clock near the bed is a little detail that goes a long way for weary travelers who don't happen to wear watches.

take back the party

Parties are such a perfect opportunity to show off our sensual leanings, aren't they? We manipulate the lighting, the décor, the aromas wafting out from our kitchen and special-events candles, the sounds, and the overall ambiance.

Parties are mini fantasies, offering our guests a brief escape from everyday living in the comforts of our nest. Too often, though, the stress of hosting an event gets in the way of our own enjoyment of the party. And when the host is stressed out, well, so sometimes are the guests. Creating the mood and experience you desire requires diligent planning, prepping, and a few up-the-sleeve tips from those who are natural hosts.

The Guest List

A successful party always starts with the guest list, since the degree of interaction among guests is really what makes or breaks a gathering. To come up with the perfect mix of people, you first need to assess your space and determine how many heads it will comfortably accommodate for mixing and mingling. Invite a number that will not crowd your place, but *will* fill it up adequately.

"The most important factor is to determine the party-list size and keep it in tune with the expectations and tone of your party," says Angela, thirty-four, from Houston. "The worst parties I've been to are those that look like the host wanted it to be a wild dance party and there were only ten people standing around looking uncomfortable while the strobe lights flashed and the bass beat thumped—or the converse, sixty people trying to use the 'make your own appletini' bar in the corner of the tiny kitchen."

If you live in a tiny studio that only holds six (max) for a sit-down dinner around your coffee table, don't try to host Thanksgiving for twelve of your closest friends. When it comes to eating, everyone wants a comfortable spot to rest their plate and drink, as well as elbow room for cutting turkey, no matter how riveting the conversation.

Offer to be the chef at your friend's airy beach house instead, and cohost the fall feast there. Face it, your nest is probably better suited for intimate champagne/dessert gatherings or cocktail parties where guests are dressed to vamp—not eat a pound of rich, gravy-soaked food. Think Holly Golightly. And save the sit-downs for a few lucky guests at a time.

In addition to size, it's important to consider the mix of personalities when you come up with your A-list. In all of my interviewing, the general consensus was to avoid mixing up groups of friends unless you have a very large party, such as a BBQ, "where a critical mass is important," as one interviewee put it.

There are many reasons to avoid mixing groups. For one, they may separate upon arrival. At one of her parties, Justine, thirty-one, from Mountain View, California, noticed that everyone divided up by career: "The designers were in the bedroom, the architects staked out the living room, and the random computer programmer/biotech sorts claimed the kitchen," she recalls. "Since then, we try not to mix industries too much."

Also, if you invite everyone who works in the same industry aside from one or two others who work in completely different fields, the conversation will likely be dominated by the shared interests of the larger group, which is often a bore for the one or two infiltrators. When this happens, you as host will end up trying too hard to keep the outsiders involved in the conversation and you'll end up feeling guilty and obligated and exhausted by the end of the evening.

Sarah, thirty-six, from Kailua, Hawaii, plans her guest lists using the following rules: (1) "Gather folk who are in the same situation—they have kids or are interested in having kids, they work their asses off to save the world, or they're doing whatever they can not to work their asses off." (2) "Don't assume people want to or have the time to see beyond their differences to get to know each other. Save that guest list for your wedding, and then never again!" (3) "Only invite the boring people with their mutual friends; don't add them to a larger mix."

In defense of boring people, though, I'd like to add that we all know a few of them and love them for their exceptional qualities, which don't happen to include socializing at parties. Joanna, thirty-one, from Los Angeles, suggests inviting only two to four wallflowers per party because "a room full of wallflowers is no fun and there will be no one to break the ice."

To avoid the separation issue, consider smaller parties for specific groups. That's what Maria, thirty, from Brooklyn, New York, does. "I never mix friends because it always makes me feel pressured to

---

🐦 **Go-Girl Guidance** 🐦

"At my parties, I put out a half-finished jigsaw puzzle on the coffee table so fidgety people and guys with no social skills will have something to do."

—*Lana, twenty-nine, from Los Angeles*

make sure everyone has things to talk about and I don't want to feel like I'm babying my thirty-year-old friends." For her housewarming, she had one party for friends from high school and the neighborhood, a second party for family, and a third for work friends. "Why bother trying to be all those things at one party?" she says.

Isabelle, thirty-one, from Sacramento, California, keeps her get-togethers small for the same reason: "I used to try to mix my friends with my husband's friends, thinking that everyone would mingle and have interesting conversations, but that never happened. My friends would gather in one room to talk and my husband's friends would bond in another. So we keep our parties small so we can concentrate on our guests in a more intimate setting," she says.

One other consideration in terms of the mix is bringing the singles together with the couples. It's never fun to be the only singleton at a party filled with couples. "Being single more often than not, I have too many anecdotes of coupled-out parties, and I no longer attend certain people's parties because I know what to expect," says Olivia, thirty-one, from Berkeley, California. For that reason, she always tries to create a nice balance in her own gatherings.

Joanna agrees that this type of mixing is important for a party's success. While her circle includes mostly couples, she always invites three to four single people: "They break up the couple unit dynamic and having each other is good so they won't feel like they are the only single people on Earth."

Angela, thirty-four, from Houston, puts it this way: "All-couples is as dull as church. All-singles is a little freaky and contrived, especially as we grow older." Tammy, thirty, from San Francisco, always makes a point of inviting enough single guys to go around at her parties. "Invite a handful of single, cute, fun, and sexy guys to your gatherings and your single girlfriends will sing your praises for weeks," she says.

Occasionally, mixing up the crowd with abandon works beautifully—especially at larger parties. Angela strives for a seventy/thirty mix of folk who know each other well/don't know each other, and with some exceptions, tries not to worry too much about whether or not people will mesh. "I am blessed with smart, interesting, openminded, and kind friends. I figure that if I like them well enough to have them over, they can be trusted to behave. If someone is suffering from The Dulls, well, so be it."

Olivia creates her own special balance by inviting no more than two "outsiders" per set of friends, unless it is either a huge party (in which case everyone's on their own) or an "all set" party (in which everyone is from the same group) or an "all set" with only one outsider "who then becomes your adoptee," she says, "which only works for a dinner party."

The Party Prep

In addition to the well-conceived guest list, a party is only as successful as it is well planned. A properly prepped party runs with fewer mishaps than the last-minute "come on over," which can be slightly stressful if you are a perfectionist or don't know the guests all that well.

Guests feel special and taken care of when the party has been thoroughly preplotted. Attending a well-conceived party feels like a momentary escape from everyday reality. You typically don't have a feeling of not knowing what to do with yourself because the well-conceived party makes it clear what your job as guest is to do: grab a drink and socialize or roll up your sleeves and make your own pizza before the game begins or simply bask in the sun on the deck while sipping mint-adorned drinks. When the focus is clear, you'll be sure to have repeat visitors at your next affair.

Planning not only involves sending out invitations with enough advance notice to ensure healthy attendance, but also requires coming up with a special menu of beverages and snacks, a theme perhaps, and a general plan for the way the party will progress. Let's discuss the major points in planning and prepping, shall we?

Invitations. A well-conceived party begins with the invitation, and there are several degrees of formality to consider these days. The snail-mail invitation on thick, textured paper holds the most authority, in my opinion, because the host is not only investing time, thought, and money on the invite, but is also taking the time to write out addresses and mail them in advance. Somehow, it just seems like a more thought-out affair when you receive an invitation in the mail.

Of course, an email invitation or a phone call is also a perfectly acceptable way to invite your near and dear to a party, especially for large or informal gatherings. But it just seems that it's easier for the recipient to forget these types of invitations because we jot them down on scraps of paper by the phone, or never transfer the evite onto our calendar, and then suddenly the party is over before we even RSVP.

Regardless of the type of invitation you choose, you'll want to send it to your guests with enough time for them to save the date and to prepare if, for instance, you are planning a theme that requires a costume or asks guests to come with a particular dish.

For special events, like a bridal shower or any birthday with a zero on the end, send the invitation three to four weeks in advance— you'll likely have a larger turnout that way. For more informal get-togethers, a couple of weeks ahead of time should do.

Nibbles and booze. Every party must have some type of food and beverage to serve your guests. That is standard custom in our country, at least. The more exotic your menu, the better. By exotic, I don't mean wild chanterelle soufflé and lychee tarts. I mean that what you serve should be somewhat out of the ordinary, different from what you and your guests likely eat every day. Serving foods one normally only eats during special occasions is an easy way to say, "Hey, it means a lot to me that you came, and so I want to treat you to something special."

If you are a real foodie, the menu will be the main attraction of your parties. It is what you most enjoy about the planning and prepping, and also what consumes most of your party-planning energy. For her parties, Claire, thirty-five, from Bellingham, Washington, spends hours poring over cookbooks and magazines, researching recipes. She centers her dinner parties around a special or seasonal dish or a theme. She also serves "nibbles" with predinner cocktails, but not so many that her guests fill up.

Sally, twenty-nine, from New York City, always includes one recipe that "steals the show" at her dinner parties. With that, she mixes less exotic offerings. And she always has an interesting mixed drink that most of her guests have not had before. For a derby party, for instance, she served mint juleps.

Kasey, twenty-five, from Hoboken, New Jersey, also makes a point to serve a fabulous drink at her gatherings. "Always have a totally self-sufficient bar and a specialty drink that you can make way beforehand and just keep replacing from the fridge," she suggests. "That makes the party very fun for guests who can just serve themselves, and it's easy for you to host."

Don't be shy about serving premade foods. Tammy, thirty, from San Francisco, California, loves to cook for her guests and has become quite famous for her soul food–inspired meals like fried fish, fried chicken, and collard greens. Still, she isn't ashamed to admit that she mixes up the homemade goods with store-bought treats. "When you mix them up on the same table, no guest will ever know the difference," she says.

Managing the menu is tricky for larger gatherings, and for that reason Olivia, thirty-one, from Berkeley, California, rarely plans a complicated menu for guests over four and never cooks difficult meals for guests she's not well acquainted with. For larger affairs, she likes using colorful vegetables for appetizers and tries to pass both hot and cold "bitings" only at set intervals so she can relax and enjoy her guests between intervals.

Angela, thirty-four, from Houston, follows these guidelines in her menu planning: "Make sure your menu is a complementary mix of sweet and salty, hot and cold, crunchy and creamy, meat and veggies. Then, mix up the colors." With this spread, every guest finds something he or she will remember.

Go-Girl Guidance

Real wineglasses can really jazz up a party. If you only have a few, consider distributing those around to reliable guests, which is what Olivia, thirty-one, from Berkeley, California, does. "It gives off a festive air," she says.

Or, consider going in on a large set with a friend, recommends Lana, twenty-nine, from Los Angeles. "Together, my friend and I bought three dozen wineglasses from a restaurant supply shop and we each store half. During parties, we get the whole set for a few weeks. Real glass is far classier than plastic."

For larger, less formal gatherings, plan on three drinks and six small "bitings" per person, advises Olivia, who also reckons, unless indications suggest otherwise, that about 70 percent of her assumed attendees will actually make the event. If in doubt about how much food to supply, go the extra mile and overstock the fridge. You can always give away plates of leftovers—your guests won't mind. And having leftovers sure beats running out of food when you have a roomful of hungry guests staring down the almost-empty plate of crudités.

Also, consider preparing some of the food in advance, when possible. For big bashes, Lana, twenty-nine, from Los Angeles, starts cooking three weeks in advance—she makes icing and freezes it for the cake. Ditto with tapenade, which she plans for baguette slices. She downplays meat and plays up produce and bread, which is easier to prep last minute and food that doesn't need to be heated. Even baked goods can be made ahead of time and frozen, thawed out several hours before the event. Your guests will never be the wiser.

In a pinch, give yourself three days—one to get the goods, one to clean the house, and one to prepare the fixings.

Final preparations. First comes the shopping, then the food prep, for which you should allot adequate time (anywhere from several weeks prior to the date to a couple of days). Claire, thirty-five, from Bellingham, Washington, usually writes up a schedule for herself a week in advance to help her prep. "I take each recipe, divide the ingredients into categories about where to shop for them—Safeway for canned or bottled items, a nicer market for veggies and meat, a cheese shop, and other specialties stores," she says. "The most difficult thing is being realistic about what you can accomplish in a given amount of time."

Don't forget to budget in time for cleaning the house (and stashing away any items you may not wish your guests to see or anything of particular value . . . in case that sketchy friend-of-a-friend goes poking around). Joanna, thirty-one, from Los Angeles, spends two full days before the party cooking and cleaning, while Amanda, twenty-seven, from Chicago, always cleans the morning of, saving the kitchen and bathroom for last, after the food is made and she's taken a shower. Another approach is to do a rigorous cleaning the week before, with spot-check cleaning the day of.

Once clean, your nest is ready for the decorative touches that announce it's party time, including the rearranging you may need to do to accommodate the expected number of attendees. On this latter note, you'll want to move any furniture that inhibits circulation and add extra chairs if needed.

Pushing a dining-room table to the wall and setting it up buffet style is one trick. So is bringing in fold-out chairs. But if you really want your guests to mingle, don't offer a chair for every guest—that not only would take up too much room, but would also ensure that everyone is more static than fluid, and your guests may get stuck talking to people they don't want to. Unless you're planning a sit-down dinner, keep the ratio of one chair to approximately every three-to-five guests. Floor pillows is a nice option, if you have them, because they are so portable and cozy and have a sense of informality to them.

To facilitate circulation, always separate the food and drinks so everyone isn't clumped up in a huddle trying to get at the goods. Spread the offerings around the room in several spots, and even divide the food into different rooms—the kitchen island, the living-room coffee table, the dining-room sidebar. If you have an outdoor deck, even better—set up the bar out there. This will keep your guests circulating and spaced evenly around your nest. What's more, this kind of separation ensures that if there are guests within the group who don't talk to each other, they can stick to their territory without causing a scene.

OVERCOMING PREPARTY ANGST

Most of us get some degree of it. Here are ways to get over it once and for all.

"I focus on the little things—arranging the hors d'oeuvres nicely, vacuuming the carpet, cleaning the mirrors. That takes the focus away from those larger 'what if everyone thinks I suck' feelings."   —*Amanda, twenty-seven, from Chicago*

"Choose your outfit a few days before!"
     —*Madison, twenty-eight, from Westfield, New Jersey*

"Remind yourself that your friends love you and don't care if everything is perfect. They just want to spend time with you."
     —*Joanna, thirty-one, from Los Angeles*

"I tell a few people that the start is a little earlier than the actual start so they come on time and the rest of your guests feel like they are walking into something that is 'happening.'"
     —*Drew, thirty-three, from New Hartford, New York*

> "One hour before, stop what you are doing and make sure you are on schedule to be dressed and ready yourself. Thirty minutes before the party, stop and adjust the lighting, put on music and pour yourself a glass of wine."
> —*Angela, thirty-four, from Houston*

> "I always try to eat an early dinner before the party and have a drink the first hour while waiting for people to show up. That way you don't get drunk at your own party and can still have fun."
> —*Alice, thirty-four, from San Diego*

Hosting 101

The final step to welcoming the flock is doing just that: welcoming. The job responsibilities of a host are really quite simple: warming up to the guests, making introductions and facilitating conversations, mastering the ceremony (that is, directing the flow of party events), and keeping the food and drinks flowing.

Always have an idea in the back of your head of how you would like the party to progress when your guests arrive, especially if your party has a focus. For instance, at a baby shower, you might plan for one hour of mingling with drinks and finger food. Then, a couple of games or activities to warm up the gaggle of girls and get everyone interacting as a group. Nondorky example: Steer your guests toward a watercolor station, where you've set up several pieces of blank paper and paints—the works of art your guests create become offerings for the baby's nursery (or at least can be hung up on the walls of the hospital room during the new mom's recovery).

Next on the agenda: opening gifts and devouring that gorgeous cake that's been vamping on the dining-room table. Then, the farewells. Before you know it, the party is over and the transition from event to event seemed seamless—because the events were so well shepherded by the host.

If the party has no theme other than "cocktails" or "tea time" or, simply, "dinner," you'll want to make the main event the focal point of the party. Lead up to it with mingling or even an activity. If dinner is the cause, serve your guests related appetizers for the first hour. If it's a super-informal affair, involve them in the salad making or dessert shaping. This is very un-French of me to suggest, but then I'm an American despite my last name, and informality is a key component of most of my parties.

Aside from having a general plan on how the party will shape up, welcoming the guests is always a sign of proper hosting. Taking hats and coats and walking your guests through your nest, pointing out the highlights (here's the food, here's the bar, oh, and here's Rebecca!) is a good start.

Before dropping that guest into the void, though, always find a mutual friend and bring the two together. If the person is a new friend who knows no one else, have a plan for him or her beforehand. Either keep that guest by your side until he or she warms up to the crowd, or have another guest in mind that you might pair that guest up with due to a common interest: rock climbing, knitting, traveling to Bali.

Either case, it's always helpful to drop-kick a conversation starter, if you can. "Hey, guess what? Mary just got a new job!" Then, once the two take the bait, excuse yourself and hurry back to the front door, because more guests are letting themselves in, and you'll want to be the one to greet them.

One of the hardest parts of hosting is keeping your guests filled to the brim with food and drinks while welcoming others. Once your guests have all arrived, one of your main concerns becomes replenishing the goods as they begin to dwindle. Since it is almost impossible to do this single-handedly, it's always smart to ask a friend or two to help with the replenishing, the music, the greeting in a pinch, as well as the socializing. Not only will your party flow, but you will not have to spend the entire event in the kitchen mixing dip and making margaritas.

You might even consider hiring a high school or college student to help, especially in serving food and keeping the kitchen tidy, doing dishes along the way. With this kind of assistance, you might even get to enjoy the party yourself, showing off your nesting instincts without worrying about every little detail. Remember, the key to good hosting is to make your guests feel special and loved and pampered. You can't do that with your hands in the sink drowning in Palmolive.

Also, keep in mind that a little chaos isn't always a bad thing. "Chaos puts people at ease," says Abby, twenty-six, from Woodbury, Connecticut. "I think it actually makes the party better because nothing is too perfect," she says.

That is true, I would agree, only if the host is relaxed about the chaos. There's nothing worse than a stressed-out host. It makes the guests feel like they should be doing something to help out, which is hardly relaxing or fun.

Laura, thirty-two, from Warren, Michigan, says the key to good hosting is to just relax and not get wrapped up in small things that go wrong. "Know that those who mind don't matter," she says, "and those who matter don't mind." A fine mantra to live by for any occasion in which you open up your nest to others, I might add.

Epilogue:
Nesting for Two (or More)

If you have roommates, sharing your nest is probably old hat. The longer you live with a friend, flat mate, family member, or lover, the better equipped you'll be at sharing the often complicated and creative tasks of building and decorating a nest for two. Those of you about to enter that stage in life, it may behoove you to be aware of the challenges now, for sharing a nest can be quite a struggle when you and your mate have different nesting instincts and ideas for what constitutes "home."

When those struggles arise, you may have come up with some solutions for dealing with disagreements: "You decorate the living room, and I'll take the den." Or, "We'll paint two walls your color, two walls mine." One interior designer I interviewed said that she had a client, a married couple, who went as far as building a tree house in the backyard so the husband could have his own private space to decorate fully on this own. Not a bad idea, if you ask me. If only all the people in the world could have tree houses.

When you're nesting with another—especially if that other person is new to a nest you've already built for yourself, or if you are starting from scratch in a new home, compromise is important, of course, but so is carving out some private nesting space for yourself. Even if that's just a corner in a room.

For Drew, thirty-three, from New Hartford, New York, that means a table in the bedroom, which she covered with a red silk cloth. "It acts like a little personal altar with a statue of Buddha, a deck of tarot cards, incense, and a painting I made," she says.

Jasmine, twenty-nine, from Long Island, New York, stakes the spare bedroom, where her closet is, when she needs time to reflect. "We have a bed in there and I can relax when my boyfriend is downstairs and I need some space. He respects when I go in there for personal time," she says.

When sharing a nest, there's another thing to keep in mind: Nesting is an active verb. There is nothing static about turning a house into a home, because we are constantly evolving and forming new ideas for making our homes perfectly catered to our sensual yearnings.

When we travel to foreign countries, we often get new ideas for dressing up our nest or making it more of a haven than it already is. Feather comforters in Germany? What bedding could possibly be more appropriate than a down comforter? A no-shoe policy in the house, as is the custom of so many cultures around the world, from Japan to Norway? How better to keep the nest clean! Coffee and dessert around the coffee table (not the dining table) after a long meal, as is the tradition in Prague? What a relaxed way to savor the end of a meal!

And then, of course, there's the subject of babies and what they do to our nesting instincts (don't even get me started!). When I was pregnant, which is actually when I began formulating ideas for this book, I was a maniac nester: organizing the closets, throwing things out, making curtains, and decorating the nursery.

While having a baby hasn't been the only life event to trigger my nesting instincts—a job promotion jump-started those impulses once, marriage again, and buying my first home really brought them out of the closet—something about welcoming a baby into your home has a way of throwing all nesters into a tizzy.

Nesting is a lifelong obsession, and ever evolving. I hope this book has given you some ideas to get you started. Enjoy the flight, for there really is no place like home.

Resources

CHAPTER 1

Decorating for Good: A Step-by-Step Guide to Rearranging What You Already Own by Carole Talbott (Clarkson N. Potter/Random House, 1999)

Use What You Have Decorating: Transform Your Home in One Hour with 10 Simple Design Principles Using the Space You Have, the Things You Like, the Budget You Choose by Lauri Ward (Perigree, 1999)

CHAPTER 3

Elfa Space and Storage Solutions: http://www.elfa.com/index.cfm?sprakid=2

California Closets: http://calclosets.com/

CHAPTER 4

Home Trends Catalogue: 800-810-2340 or http://www.hometrend
  scatalog.com (excellent resource for household cleaning products
  and organizing gadgets)
Home Comforts: The Art & Science of Keeping House by Cheryl
  Mendelson (Scribner, 1999)

CHAPTER 5

Colors for Your Every Mood: Discover Your True Decorating Colors by
  Leatrice Eiseman (Capital Books, 1998)
Choosing a Color Scheme (Creative Homeowner Press, 1992)
Stenciling resources: The Stencil Library http://www.stencil-
  library.com/; Designer Stencils: http://www.designerstencils.
  com/; L.A. Stencilworks: http://www. lastencil.com/; Bucking-
  ham Stencils; http://buckinghamstencils.com/store. asp; Win-
  drush Designs: http://www.windrushdesigns.com/index.html;
  Epoch Designs: http://www.epochdesigns.com/

CHAPTER 6

Slipcovers: http://www.surefit.com

CHAPTER 7

The Complete Book of Floors by Alan Berman (Frances Lincoln,
  1997)
Design within Reach (floor tiles and more): http://www.dwr.com/
Interface (Flor tiles): 866-281-FLOR; http://www.interfaceflor.
  com/service/flor/index.html

CHAPTER 8

Ideas for Great Home Lighting by Scott Atkinson (Sunset Publishing, 2003)

The Complete Home Lighting Book: Contemporary Interior & Exterior Lighting for the Home by James Davidson (Overlook Press, 1997)

CHAPTER 9

What Houseplants Where by Roy Lancaster and Matthew Biggs (DK Publishing, 1998)

Decorating with Plants by Oliver Allen and the editors of Time-Life Books (Time-Life Books, 1978)

Displaying Pictures and Photographs by Caroline Clifton-Mogg and Piers Feetham (Crown, 1988)

OTHER

American Society of Interior Designers (ASID: 202-467-1950; http://www.asid. org/

International Interior Design Association: 888-799-4432; http://www. iida.org

Index